THE IDLER'S COMPANION

the *Idler's* *Companion*

AN ANTHOLOGY OF LAZY LITERATURE

Edited by

Tom Hodgkinson &
Matthew DeAbaitua

THE ECCO PRESS

THE ECCO PRESS
100 West Broad Street
Hopewell, New Jersey 08525

Printed in the United States of America

LIBRARY OF CONGRESS CATALOGING-IN-PUBLICATION DATA
The idler's companion : an anthology of lazy literature / edited by
Tom Hodgkinson and Matthew De Abaitua. – 1st Ecco ed.
p.   cm.
ISBN 0-88001-549-7
1. Laziness – Literary collections. I. Hodgkinson, Tom. II. De Abaitua,
Matthew, 1971- .
PN6071.L37I35   1997
808.8'0353 – dc21   97-9463

Designed by Susanna Gilbert, The Typeworks
The text of this book is set in Spectrum

9 8 7 6 5 4 3 2 1

FIRST EDITION 1997

CONTENTS

the Monk

the Unemployed

INTRODUCTION

What is an idler? The word is most commonly used these days in its pejorative sense: an idler is lazy, a good-for-nothing, a layabout, slacker, indole, a slothful couch potato who contributes nothing to society, a sponging lollygag without the wherewithal and discipline to put in an honest day's toil. This, at least, is the orthodox view.

It is our belief, however, and one which is demonstrated repeatedly in this book, that idleness has a rich and noble heritage dating back centuries. Idleness is seen again and again for what it actually is: a rejection of worldly pressures, an individualist revolt against authority, a pleasure, a spiritual practice. The work ethic is revealed as a relatively recent phenomenon, conceived to make people slave away in dark satanic mills for puny returns.

An idler, you will find, is not a regrettable drain on society, but, in fact, a veritable saint. Idlers are a pure and noble breed.

At the inception of the anthology, we felt that the history of idleness was a hidden history, not as well documented as overt rebellion, as its objections to society were insinuations rather than revolutions. However, after much research we learned that this was not the case: countless meditations on doing nothing have been printed; endless calls for the end of the cult of work have been filed; innumerable sick days have been wangled, tools have been downed, feet have kicked back – all, it seems, when one looks around at the frenetic commuters and barked phone calls of the metropolis, in vain. Yet, in the words of Joad, "the victories of the mind and spirit have to be won afresh in every age."

It was with such victories in mind that *The Idler* magazine was founded in 1993. Its intent was to combine the hidden history of indolence with the reflections of its more recent advocates. Those who were coming of age as the Eighties dissolved into so many broken materialistic dreams found themselves in a work culture bedeviled by spurious management theories and bowed, insecure staff. The youth culture that had worried at its cuticles over the range of careers promised by a Thatcherite culture of success learned quickly that these were not choices open to just anyone (and certainly not to a "just-about-someone" like ourselves), and that the fractal of possibilities was, in fact, an alleyway leading from menial education to menial employment.

We assembled this anthology in the hope that the combined inertia of all this lazy literature would finally push the Sisyphian boulder of change over the hill, and we could all trundle happily down the grassy slope of the rest of our lives. Which would be some victory. In the meantime, we console ourselves with the one piece of advice that permeates throughout idle thought: do nothing. Do nothing that offends you, at least. Let events resolve themselves. The hours of research we put in at the British Library yielded a minimum of material; the off-hand telephone inquiry, the randomly browsed volume, the bookshop where the relevant works seemed to leap off the shelves and into our hands – it was out of these serendipitous sources that the collection was hewn.

Kick back,

MDA & TH
Clerkenwell, London 1996.

ACKNOWLEDGMENTS

This anthology would not have been possible without the help, support and inspiration provided by those who have contributed to *The Idler* magazine. So to all of you, writers, designers, photographers, illustrators and, of course, readers, many thanks.

Needless to say, when assembling this anthology, we relied upon the expertise and knowledge of others. Marcel Theroux, Mark Sanders, Matt ffytche, David Brook, Will Self, Dan Glaister, Robert Hanks, Suzanne Moore, Charles Handy, Damien Hirst, Terence McKenna, Victoria Coren, Joshua Glenn, Simon Jameson, Dean at AK, Oliver Curry, Cathy Wilson and Cathy Wheeler all provided essential material. We would also like to thank Sally Holloway for her cajoling, her calm demeanor and her patience.

The extract from *Cain's Book* by Alexander Trocchi is reprinted by permission of the Alexander Trocchi Estate and the Calder Educational Trust, London. Copyright © Alexander Trocchi 1960 and copyright © Sally Childs 1992. The extract from *Oblomov* by Ivan Goncharov, trans. Natalie Duddington, 1932, reprinted by permission of Everyman's Library, David Campbell Publishers Ltd. Extract from *Opium* by Jean Cocteau, translated by Margaret Crosland, by permission of Peter Owen Ltd, London. Extract from *The Importance of Living* by Lin Yutang, published by William Heinemann, by permission of Reed Books Ltd. Extract from Who Will Do The Dirty Work by Tony Gibson from *Why Work?* by permission of Freedom Press, 84b Whitechapel High Street, Lon-

tion copyright © Richard Howard 1977. The extract from *Lost Horizon* by James Hilton, copyright © James Hilton, is reproduced by permission of Curtis Brown Group Ltd, London. The extract from *Ethics* of Aristotle, trans. J.A.K. Thomson, reproduced by permission of Routledge (Allen & Unwin, 1953). The extract from *Future Work* by James Robertson reproduced with permission of the author © James Robertson. Eight Miles High by Will Self copyright © Will Self. Labor of Love by Suzanne Moore copyright © Suzanne Moore.

Where written permission has not been obtained, every effort has been made by the editors to contact the holder of the copyright. We will be happy to rectify any omissions in future editions of the book, and copyright holders are welcome to write to us c/o the publisher.

THE IDLER'S COMPANION

the Courtier

"I prefer not to." It was with this elegant refusal that Melville's Bartleby turned his back on the working life.

Not all scriveners are so confident in their rebuttals of endeavor as him, however. Dr. Samuel Johnson was particularly ambivalent over his inability to rise early, writing being a profession particularly susceptible to guilt about procrastination: there are always further revisions, greater research, more pages to be filled to overcome the imprecise translation of thought to thesis.

The paradox of idleness lies in the productivity of its advocates; the writer who lounges hookah in hand for weeks can suddenly snap — like the sudden contraction of an over-extended elastic band — into a period of frenzied activity. We begin this anthology with the testaments of such idlers, all respected men of letters, who found themselves divided between the ivory tower of contemplation and the need to be out, on the streets, buried headfirst in the pursuits of the people. They are courtiers, who compose their love letters to a vice.

———◆———

The Idler, No. 1

SAMUEL JOHNSON, 1758

In 1758, a successful Samuel Johnson began contributing a twice weekly essay, under the name of The Idler, to a magazine called the Universal Chronicle, *and at a stroke defined a state of mind. Here we reproduce the first of those essays.*

Vacui sub umbra
Lusimus.

HORACE

*T*hose who attempt periodical essays seem to be often stopped in the beginning, by the difficulty of finding a proper title. Two writers, since the time of the Spectator, have assumed his name, without any pretensions to lawful inheritance; an effort was once made to revive the Tatler; and the strange appellations, by which other papers have been called, show that the authors were distressed, like the natives of America, who come to the Europeans to beg a name.

It will be easily believed of the Idler, that if his title had required any search, he never would have found it. Every mode of life has its conveniences. The Idler, who habituates himself to be satisfied with what he can most easily obtain, not only escapes labors which are often fruitless, but sometimes succeeds better than those who despise all that is within their reach, and think every thing more valuable as it is harder to be acquired.

If similitude of manners be a motive to kindness, the Idler may flatter himself with universal patronage. There is no single character under which such numbers are comprised. Every man is, or hopes to be, an Idler. Even those who seem to differ most from us are hastening to increase our fraternity; as peace is the end of war, so to be idle is the ultimate purpose of the busy.

There is perhaps no appellation by which a writer can better denote his kindred to the human species. It has been found hard to describe man by an adequate definition. Some philosophers have called him a reasonable animal; but others have considered reason as a quality of which many creatures partake. He has been termed likewise a laughing animal; but it is said that some men have never laughed. Perhaps man may be more properly distinguished as an idle animal; for there is no man who is not sometimes idle. It is at least a definition from which none that shall find it in this paper can be excepted; for who can be more idle than the reader of the Idler?

That the definition may be complete, idleness must be not only the general, but the peculiar characteristic of man; and perhaps man is the only being that can properly be called idle, that does by others what he might do himself, or sacrifices duty or pleasure to the love of ease.

Scarcely any name can be imagined from which less envy or competition is to be dreaded. The Idler has no rivals or enemies. The man of business forgets him; the man of enterprise despises him; and though such as tread the same track of life fall commonly into jealousy and discord, Idlers are always found to associate in peace; and he who is most famed for doing nothing, is glad to meet another as idle as himself.

What is to be expected from this paper, whether it will be uniform or various, learned or familiar, serious or gay, political or moral, continued or interrupted, it is hoped that no reader will enquire. That the Idler has some scheme, cannot be doubted, for to form schemes is the

Idler's privilege. But though he has many projects in his head, he is now grown sparing of communication, having observed, that his hearers are apt to remember what he forgets himself; that his tardiness of execution exposes him to the encroachments of those who catch a hint and fall to work; and that very specious plans, after long contrivance and pompous displays, have subsided in weariness without a trial, and without miscarriage have been blasted by derision.

Something the Idler's character may be supposed to promise. Those that are curious after diminutive history, who watch the revolutions of families, and the rise and fall of characters either male or female, will hope to be gratified by this paper; for the Idler is always inquisitive and seldom retentive. He that delights in obloquy and satire, and wishes to see clouds gathering over any reputation that dazzles him with its brightness, will snatch up the Idler's essays with a beating heart. The Idler is naturally censorious; those who attempt nothing themselves, think every thing easily performed, and consider the unsuccessful always as criminal.

I think it necessary to give notice, that I make no contract, nor incur any obligation. If those who depend on the Idler for intelligence and entertainment, should suffer the disappointment which commonly follows ill-placed expectations, they are to lay the blame only on themselves.

Yet hope is not wholly to be cast away. The Idler, though sluggish, is yet alive, and may sometimes be stimulated to vigor and activity. He may descend into profoundness, or tower into sublimity; for the diligence of an Idler is rapid and impetuous, as ponderous bodies forced into velocity move with violence proportionate to their weight.

But these vehement exertions of intellect cannot be frequent, and he will therefore gladly receive help from any correspondent, who shall enable him to please without his own labor. He excludes no style, he prohibits no subject; only let him that writes to the Idler remember, that his letters must not be long; no words are to be squandered in declarations of esteem, or confessions of inability; conscious dullness has little right to be prolix, and praise is not so welcome to the Idler as quiet.

⟶⟵

from *Oblomov*

IVAN GONCHAROV, 1859

Oblomov is well known as the laziest hero of Russian literature. Here Goncharov describes his protagonist's love for his dressing-gown.

The dressing-gown had a number of invaluable qualities in Oblomov's eyes: it was soft and pliable; it did not get in his way; it obeyed the least movement of his body, like a docile slave.

Oblomov never wore a tie or waistcoat at home because he liked comfort and freedom. He wore long, soft, wide slippers; when he got up from bed he put his feet straight into them without looking.

Lying down was not for Ilya Ilyitch either a necessity as it is for a sick or a sleepy man, or an occasional need as it is for a person who is tired, or a pleasure as it is for a sluggard: it was his normal state. When he was at home — and he was almost always at home — he was lying down, and invariably in the same room, the one in which we have found him and which served him as bedroom, study, and reception-room. He had three more rooms, but he seldom looked into them, only, perhaps, in the morning when his servant swept his study — which did not happen every day. In those other rooms the furniture was covered and the curtains were drawn.

———

from *Cain's Book*
ALEXANDER TROCCHI, 1960

Lauded by the Beats, Trocchi never truly fulfilled his formidable promise as a writer. Here he praises the pleasures of play, and in particular playing pinball.

*I*n early life sensations like metaphysical burglars burst forcibly in(to) the living. In early life things strike with the magic of their existence. The creative moment comes out of the past with some of the magic unimpaired; involvement in it is impossible for an attitude of compromise. Nevertheless it is not the power to abstract that is invalid, but the unquestioning acceptance of conventional abstractions which stand in the way of raw memory, of the existential . . . all such barriers to the gradual refinement of the central nervous system.

It is not a question simply of allowing the volcano to erupt. A burnt backside is not going to help anyone. And the ovens of Auschwitz are scarcely cold. When the spirit of play dies there is only murder.

Play. *Homo ludens.*

Playing pinball for example in a café called le Grap d'Or.

In the pinball machine an absolute and peculiar order reigns. No skepticism is possible for the man who by a series of sharp and slight dunts tries to control the machine. It became for me a ritual act, symbolizing a cosmic event. Man is serious at play. Tension, elation, frivolity, ecstasy, confirming the supra-logical nature of the human situation. Apart from jazz — probably the most vigorous and yea-saying protest of *homo ludens* in the modern world — the pinball machine seemed to me to be America's greatest contribution to culture; it rang with contemporaneity. It symbolized the rigid structural "soul" that threatened to crystallize in history, reducing man to historicity, the great mechanic monolith imposed by mass mind; it symbolized it and reduced it to nothing. The slick electric shiftings of the pinball machine, the electronic brain, the symbolical transposition of the modern Fact into the realm of play. (The distinction between the French and the American attitude towards the "tilt" ("teelt"); in America, and England, I have been upbraided for trying to beat the mechanism by skillful tilting; in Paris, that is the whole point.)

Man is forgetting how to play. Yes, we have taught the mass that work is sacred, hard work. Now that the man of the mass is coming into his own he threatens to reimpose the belief we imposed on him. The men of no tradition "dropped into history through a trapdoor" in a short space of 150 years were never taught to play, were never told that their work was "sacred" only in the sense that it enabled their masters to play.

The beauty of cricket. The vulgarity of professionalism. The anthropological treason of those who treat culture "seriously," who think in terms of educating the mass instead of teaching man how to play. The callow, learned jackanapes who trail round art exhibitions looking for they know not what in another's bright turd. How soon Dada was mummified by its inclusion in the histories.

Many of the poets and painters in Paris in the early Fifties played pinball; few, unfortunately, without feelings of guilt.

On Being Idle

JEROME K. JEROME, 1889

Jerome, author of Three Men in a Boat, *edited a magazine called* The Idler *in the 1890s. Here the inveterate indolent captures the paradox of the busy idler.*

Now this is a subject on which I flatter myself I really am *au fait*. The gentleman who, when I was young, bathed me at wisdom's font for nine guineas a term — no extras — used to say he never knew a boy who could do less work in more time; and I remember my poor grandmother once incidentally observing, in the course of an instruction upon the use of the prayer-book, that it was highly improbable that I should ever do much that I ought to do, but, that she felt convinced beyond a doubt that I should leave undone pretty well everything that I ought to do.

I am afraid I have somewhat belied half the dear old lady's prophecy. Heaven help me! I have done a good many things that I ought not to have done, in spite of my laziness. But I have fully confirmed the accuracy of her judgment so far as neglecting much that I ought not to have neglected is concerned. Idling always has been my strong point. I take no credit to myself in the matter — it is a gift. Few possess it. There are plenty of lazy people and plenty of slowcoaches, but a genuine idler is a rarity. He is not a man who slouches about with his hands in his pockets. On the contrary, his most startling characteristic is that he is always intensely busy.

It is impossible to enjoy idling thoroughly unless one has plenty of work to do. There is no fun in doing nothing when you have nothing to do. Wasting time is merely an occupation then, and a most exhausting one. Idleness, like kisses, to be sweet must be stolen.

Many years ago, when I was a young man, I was taken very ill — I never could see myself that much was the matter with me, except that I had a beastly cold. But I suppose it was something very serious, for the doctor said that I ought to have come to him a month before, and that if it (whatever it was) had gone on for another week he would not have answered for the consequences. It is an extraordinary thing, but I never knew a doctor called into any case yet, but what it transpired that another day's delay would have rendered cure hopeless. Our medical guide, philosopher, and friend is like the hero in a melodrama, he always comes upon the scene just, and only just, in the nick of time. It is Providence, that is what it is.

Well, as I was saying, I was very ill, and was ordered to Buxton for a month, with strict injunctions to do nothing whatever all the while that I was there. "Rest is what you require," said the doctor, "perfect rest."

It seemed a delightful prospect. "This man evidently understands my complaint," said I, and I pictured to myself a glorious time — a four weeks' *dolce far niente* with a dash of illness in it. Not too much illness, but just illness enough — just sufficient to give it the flavor of suffering, and make it poetical. I should get up late, sip chocolate, and have my breakfast in slippers and a dressing gown. I should lie out in the garden in a hammock, and read sentimental novels with a melancholy ending, until the book would fall from my listless hand, and I should recline there, dreamily gazing into the deep blue of the firmament, watching the fleecy clouds, floating like white-sailed ships, across its depths, and listening to the joyous song of the birds, and the low rustling of the trees. Or, when I became too weak to go out of doors, I should sit, propped up with pillows, at the open window of the ground floor front, and look wasted and interesting, so that all the pretty girls would sigh as they passed by.

And, twice a day, I should go down in a Bath chair to the Colonnade, to drink the waters. Oh, those waters! I knew nothing about them then, and was rather taken with the idea. "Drinking the waters" sounded fashionable and Queen Anneified, and I thought I should like them. But, ugh! after the first three or four mornings! Sam Weller's description of them, as "having a taste of warm flat-irons," conveys only a faint idea of their hideous nauseousness. If anything could make a sick man get well, quickly, it would be the knowledge that he must drink a glassful of them every day until he was recovered. I drank them neat for six consecutive days, and they nearly killed me; but, after then, I adopted the plan of taking a stiff glass of brandy and water immediately on the top of them, and found much relief thereby. I have been informed since, by various eminent medical gentlemen, that the alcohol must have entirely counteracted the effects of the chalybeate properties contained in the water. I am glad I was lucky enough to hit upon the right thing.

But "drinking the waters" was only a small portion of the torture I experienced during that memorable month, a month which was, without exception, the most miserable I have ever spent. During the best part of it, I religiously followed the doctor's mandate, and did nothing whatever, except moon about the house and garden, and go out for two hours a day in a Bath chair. That did break the monotony to a certain extent. There is more excitement about Bath-chairing — especially if you are not used to the exhilarating exercise — than might appear to the casual observer. A sense of danger, such as a mere outsider might not understand, is ever present to the mind of the occupant. He feels convinced every minute that the whole concern is going over, a conviction which becomes especially lively whenever a ditch or a stretch of newly macadamized road comes in sight. Every vehicle that passes he expects is going to run into him; and he never finds himself ascending or descending a hill, without immediately beginning to speculate upon his chances, supposing — as seems extremely probable — that the weak-kneed controller of his destiny should let go.

But even this diversion failed to enliven after a while, and the *ennui* became perfectly unbearable. I felt my mind giving way under it. It is not a strong mind, and I thought it would be unwise to tax it too far. So somewhere about the twentieth morning, I got up early, had a good breakfast, and walked straight to Hayfield at the foot of the Kinder Scout — a pleasant, busy, little town, reached through a lovely valley, and with two sweetly pretty women in it. At least they were sweetly pretty then; one passed me on the bridge, and, I think, smiled; and the other was standing at an open door, making an unremunerative investment of kisses upon a red-faced baby. But it is years ago, and I daresay they have both grown stout and snappish since that time.

Coming back, I saw an old man breaking stones, and it

roused such strong longing in me to use my arms, that I offered him a drink to let me take his place. He was a kindly old man, and he humored me. I went for those stones with the accumulated energy of three weeks, and did more work in half-an-hour than he had done all day. But it did not make him jealous.

Having taken the plunge, I went further and further into dissipation, going out for a long walk every morning, and listening to the band in the Pavilion every evening. But the days still passed slowly notwithstanding, and I was heartily glad when the last one came, and I was being whirled away from gouty, consumptive Buxton to London, with its stern work and life. I looked out of the carriage as we rushed through Hendon in the evening. The lurid glare overhanging the mighty city seemed to warm my heart, and, when later on, my cab rattled out of St. Pancras' station, the old familiar roar that came swelling up around me sounded the sweetest music I had heard for many a long day.

I certainly did not enjoy that month's idling. I like idling when I ought not to be idling; not when it is the only thing I have to do. That is my pig-headed nature. The time when I like best to stand with my back to the fire, calculating how much I owe, is when my desk is heaped highest with letters that must be answered by the next post. When I like to dawdle longest over my dinner, is when I have a heavy evening's work before me. And if, for some urgent reason, I ought to be up particularly early in the morning, it is then, more than at any other time, that I love to lie an extra half-hour in bed.

Ah! how delicious it is to turn over and go to sleep again: "just for five minutes." Is there any human being, I wonder, besides the hero of a Sunday-school "tale for boys," who ever gets up willingly? There are some men to whom getting up at the proper time is an utter impossibility. If eight o'clock happens to be the time that they should turn out, then they lie till half-past. If circumstances change and half-past eight becomes early enough for them, then it is nine before they can rise; they are like the statesman of whom it was said that he was always punctually half an hour late. They try all manner of schemes. They buy alarm clocks (artful contrivances that go off at the wrong time, and alarm the wrong people). They tell Sarah Jane to knock at the door and call them, and Sarah Jane does knock at the door, and does call them, and they grunt back "awri," and then go comfortably to sleep again. I knew one man who would actually get out, and have a cold bath; and even that was of no use, for, afterwards, he would jump into bed again to warm himself.

I think myself that I could keep out of bed all right, if I once got out. It is the wrenching away of the head from the pillow that I find so hard, and no amount of over-night determination makes it easier. I say to myself, after having wasted the whole evening, "Well, I won't do any more work tonight; I'll get up early tomorrow morning"; and I am thoroughly resolved to do so — then. In the morning, however, I feel less enthusiastic about the idea, and reflect that it would have been much better if I had stopped up last night. And then there is the trouble of dressing, and the more one thinks about that, the more one wants to put it off.

It is a strange thing this bed, this mimic grave, where we stretch our tired limbs, and sink away so quietly into the silence and rest. "Oh bed, oh bed, delicious bed, that heaven on earth to the weary head," as sang poor Hood, you are a kind old nurse to us fretful boys and girls. Clever and foolish, naughty and good, you take us all in your motherly lap, and hush our wayward crying. The strong man full of care — the sick man full of pain — the little maiden, sobbing for her faithless lover — like children, we lay our aching heads on your white bosom, and you gently soothe us off to by-by.

Our trouble is sore indeed, when you turn away, and will not comfort us. How long the dawn seems coming, when we cannot sleep! Oh! those hideous nights, when we toss and turn in fever and pain, when we lie, like living men among the dead, staring out into the dark hours that drift so slowly between us and the light. And oh! those still more hideous nights, when we sit by another in pain, when the low fire startles us every now and then with a falling cinder, and the tick of the clock seems a hammer, beating out the life that we are watching.

But enough of beds and bedrooms. I have kept to them too long, even for an idle fellow. Let us come out, and have a smoke. That wastes time just as well, and does not look so bad. Tobacco has been a blessing to us idlers. What the civil service clerks before Sir Walter's time found to occupy their minds with, it is hard to imagine. I attribute the quarrelsome nature of the Middle Ages young men entirely to the want of the soothing weed. They had no work to do, and could not smoke, and the consequence was they were for ever fighting and rowing. If, by any extraordinary chance, there was no war going, then they got up a deadly family feud with the next-door neighbor, and if, in spite of this, they still had a few spare moments on their hands, they occupied them with discussions as to whose sweetheart was the best looking, the arguments employed on both sides being battle-axes, clubs, etc. Questions of taste were soon decided in those days. When a twelfth-century youth fell in love, he did not take three paces backwards, gaze into her eyes, and tell her she was too beautiful to live. He said he would step outside and see about it. And if, when he got out, he met a man and broke his head – the other man's head, I mean – then that proved that his – the first fellow's girl – was a pretty girl. But if the other fellow broke *his* head – not his own, you know, but the other fellow's – the other fellow to the second fellow, that is, because of course the other fellow would only be the other fellow to him, not the first fellow, who – well, if he broke his head, then *his* girl – not the other fellow's, but the fellow who *was* the – Look here, if A broke B's head, then A's girl was a pretty girl, but if B broke A's head, then A's girl wasn't a pretty girl, but B's girl was. That was their method of conducting art criticism.

Now-a-days we light a pipe, and let the girls fight it out amongst themselves.

They do it very well. They are getting to do all our work. They are doctors, and barristers, and artists. They manage theaters, and promote swindles, and edit newspapers. I am looking forward to the time when we men shall have nothing to do but lie in bed till twelve, read two novels a day, have nice little five o'clock teas all to ourselves, and tax our brains with nothing more trying than discussions upon the latest patterns in trousers, and arguments as to what Mr. Jones's coat was made of and whether it fitted him. It is a glorious prospect – for idle fellows.

from *Enemies of Promise*

CYRIL CONNOLLY, 1938

Sloth in writers is always a symptom of an acute inner conflict, especially that laziness which renders them incapable of doing the thing which they are most looking forward to. The conflict may or may not end in disaster, but their silence is better than the over-production which must so end and slothful writers such as Johnson, Coleridge, Greville, in spite of the nodding poppies of conversation, morphia and horse-racing have more to their credit than Macaulay, Trollope or Scott. To accuse writers of being idle is a mark of envy or stupidity — La Fontaine slept continually and scarcely ever opened his mouth; Baudelaire, according to Dr. Laforgue, feared to perfect his work because he feared the incest with his mother which was his perfect fulfillment. Perfectionists are notoriously lazy and all true artistic indolence is deeply neurotic; a pain not a pleasure.

The Idler, No. 31

SAMUEL JOHNSON, 1758

In which Dr. Johnson proposes that idleness replace pride as the commonest of the human vices.

Many moralists have remarked that pride has of all human vices the widest dominion, appears in the greatest multiplicity of forms, and lies hid under the greatest variety of disguises; of disguises, which, like the moon's "veil of brightness," are both its "luster and its shade," and betray it to others, tho' they hide it from ourselves.

It is not my intention to degrade pride from this

pre-eminence of mischief, yet I know not whether idleness may not maintain a very doubtful and obstinate competition.

There are some that profess idleness in its full dignity who call themselves the "Idle," as Busiris in the play "calls himself the Proud"; who boast that they do nothing, and thank their stars that they have nothing to do; who sleep every night till they can sleep no longer, and rise only that exercise may enable them to sleep again; who prolong the reign of darkness by double curtains, and never see the sun but to "tell him how they hate his beams," whose whole labor is to vary the postures of indulgence, and whose day differs from their night but as a couch or chair differs from a bed.

These are the true and open votaries of idleness, for whom she weaves the garlands of poppies, and into whose cup she pours the waters of oblivion; who exist in a state of unruffled stupidity, forgetting and forgotten; who have long ceased to live, and at whose death the survivors can only say, that they have ceased to breathe.

But idleness predominates in many lives where it is not suspected, for being a vice which terminates in itself, it may be enjoyed without injury to others, and is therefore not watched like fraud, which endangers property, or like pride which naturally seeks its gratifications in another's inferiority. Idleness is a silent and peaceful quality, that neither raises envy by ostentation, nor hatred by opposition; and therefore no body is busy to censure or detect it.

As pride sometimes is hid under humility, idleness is often covered by turbulence and hurry. He that neglects his known duty and real employment, naturally endeavors to crowd his mind with something that may bar out the remembrance of his own folly, and does anything but what he ought to do with eager diligence, that he may keep himself in his own favor.

Some are always in a state of preparation, occupied in previous measures, forming plans, accumulating materials, and providing for the main affair. These are certainly under the secret power of idleness. Nothing is to be expected from the workman whose tools are for ever to be sought. I was once told by a great master, that no man ever excelled in painting, who was eminently curious about pencils and colors.

There are others to whom idleness dictates another expedient, by which life may be passed unprofitably away without the tediousness of many vacant hours. The art is, to fill the day with petty business, to have always something in hand which may raise curiosity, but not solicitude, and keep the mind in a state of action, but not of labor.

This art has for many years been practiced by my old friend Sober, with wonderful success. Sober is a man of strong desires and quick imagination, so exactly balanced by the love of ease, that they can seldom stimulate him to any difficult undertaking; they have, however, so much power, that they will not suffer him to lie quite at rest, and though they do not make him sufficiently useful to others, they make him at least weary of himself.

Mr. Sober's chief pleasure is conversation; there is no end of his talk or his attention; to speak or to hear is equally pleasing; for he still fancies that he is teaching or learning something, and is free for the time from his own reproaches.

But there is one time at night when he must go home, that his friends may sleep; and another time in the morning, when all the world agrees to shut out interruption. These are the moments of which poor Sober trembles at the thought. But the misery of these tiresome intervals, he has many means of alleviating. He has persuaded himself that the manual arts are undeservedly overlooked; he has observed in many trades the effects of close thought, and just ratiocination. From speculation he proceeded to practice, and supplied himself with the tools of a carpenter, with which he mended his coal-box very successfully, and which he still continues to employ, as he finds occasion.

He has attempted at other times the crafts of the shoemaker, tinman, plumber, and potter; in all these arts he has failed, and resolves to qualify himself for them by better information. But his daily amusement is chemistry. He has a small furnace, which he employs in distillation, and which has long been the solace of his life. He draws oils and waters, and essences and spirits, which he knows to be of no use; sits and counts the drops as they come from his retort, and forgets that, while a drop is falling, a moment flies away.

Poor Sober! I have often teased him with reproof, and he has often promised reformation; for no man is so much open to conviction as the idler, but there is none on whom it operates so little. What will be the effect of this paper I know not; perhaps he will read it and laugh, and light the fire in his furnace; but my hope is that he will quit his trifles, and betake himself to rational and useful diligence.

from *Bartleby the Scrivener*

HERMAN MELVILLE, 1853

Herman Melville's creation Bartleby must rank as one of the most dignified slackers in the history of literature.

A t first, Bartleby did an extraordinary quantity of writing. As if long famishing for something to copy, he seemed to gorge himself on my documents. There was no pause for digestion. He ran a day and night line, copying by sun-light and by candle-light. I should have been quite delighted with his application, had he been cheerfully industrious. But he wrote on silently, palely, mechanically.

It is, of course, an indispensable part of a scrivener's business to verify the accuracy of his copy, word by word. Where there are two or more scriveners in an office, they assist each other in this examination, one reading from the copy, the other holding the original. It is a very dull, wearisome, and lethargic affair. I can readily imagine that, to some sanguine temperaments, it would be altogether intolerable. For example, I cannot credit that the mettlesome poet, Byron, would have contentedly sat down with Bartleby to examine a law document of, say five hundred pages, closely written in a crimpy hand.

Now and then, in the haste of business, it had been my habit to assist in comparing some brief document myself, calling Turkey or Nippers for this purpose. One object I had, in placing Bartleby so handy to me behind the screen, was, to avail myself of his services on such trivial occasions. It was on the third day, I think, of his being with me, and before any necessity had arisen for having his own writing examined, that, being much hurried to complete a small affair I had in hand, I abruptly called to Bartleby. In my haste and natural expectancy of instant compliance, I sat with my head bent over the original on my desk, and my right hand sideways, and somewhat nervously extended with the copy, so that, immediately upon emerging from his retreat, Bartleby might snatch it and proceed to business without the least delay.

In this very attitude did I sit when I called to him, rapidly stating what it was I wanted him to do — namely, to examine a small paper with me. Imagine my surprise, nay, my consternation, when, without moving from his privacy, Bartleby, in a singularly mild, firm voice, replied, "I would prefer not to."

I sat awhile in perfect silence, rallying my stunned faculties. Immediately it occurred to me that my ears had deceived me, or Bartleby had entirely misunderstood my meaning. I repeated my request in the clearest tone I could assume; but in quite as clear a one came the previous reply, "I would prefer not to."

"Prefer not to," echoed I, rising in high excitement, and crossing the room with a stride. "What do you mean? Are you moonstruck? I want you to help me compare this sheet here — take it," and I thrust it towards him.

"I would prefer not to," said he.

I looked at him steadfastly. His face was leanly composed; his gray eye dimly calm. Not a wrinkle of agitation rippled him. Had there been the least uneasiness, anger, impatience or impertinence in his manner; in other words, had there been any thing ordinarily human about him, doubtless I should have violently dismissed him from the premises. But as it was, I should have as soon thought of turning my pale plaster-of-paris bust of Cicero out of doors. I stood gazing at him awhile, as he went on with his own writing, and then reseated myself at my desk. This is very strange, thought I. What had one best do? But my business hurried me: I concluded to forget the matter for the present, reserving it for my future leisure. So calling Nippers from the other room, the paper was speedily examined.

A few days after this, Bartleby concluded four lengthy documents, being quadruplicates of a week's testimony taken before me in my High Court of Chancery. It became necessary to examine them. It was an important suit, and great accuracy was imperative. Having all things arranged, I called Turkey, Nippers, and Ginger Nut, from the next room, meaning to place the four copies in the hands of my four clerks, while I should read from the original. Accordingly, Turkey, Nippers, and Ginger Nut had taken their seats in a row, each with his document in his hand, when I called to Bartleby to join this interesting group.

"Bartleby! quick, I am waiting."

I heard a slow scrape of his chair legs on the uncarpeted floor, and soon he appeared standing at the entrance of his hermitage.

"What is wanted?" said he, mildly.

"The copies, the copies," said I hurriedly. "We are going to examine them. There" — and I held towards him the fourth quadruplicate.

"I would prefer not to," he said, and gently disappeared behind the screen.

For a few moments I was turned into a pillar of salt, standing at the head of my seated column of clerks. Recovering myself, I advanced towards the screen, and demanded the reason for such extraordinary conduct.

"*Why* do you refuse?"

"I would prefer not to."

With any other man I should have flown outright into a dreadful passion, scorned all further words, and thrust him ignominiously from my presence. But there was something about Bartleby that not only strangely disarmed me, but, in a wonderful manner, touched and disconcerted me. I began to reason with him.

"These are your own copies we are about to examine. It is labor saving to you, because one examination will answer for your four papers. It is common usage. Every copyist is bound to help examine his copy. Is it not so? Will you not speak? Answer!"

"I prefer not to," he replied in a flutelike tone. It seemed to me that, while I had been addressing him, he carefully revolved every statement that I made; fully comprehended the meaning; could not gainsay the irresistible conclusion; but, at the same time, some paramount consideration prevailed with him to reply as he did.

"You are decided, then, not to comply with my request — a request made according to common usage and common sense?"

He briefly gave me to understand, that on that point my judgment was sound. Yes: his decision was irreversible.

It is not seldom the case that, when a man is browbeaten in some unprecedented and violently unreasonable way, he begins to stagger in his own plainest faith. He begins, as it were, vaguely to surmise that, wonderful as it may be, all the justice and all the reason is on the other side. Accordingly, if any disinterested persons are present, he turns to them for some reinforcement of his own faltering mind.

"Turkey," said I, "what do you think of this? Am I not right?"

"With submission, sir," said Turkey, in his blandest tone, "I think that you are."

"Nippers," said I, "what do *you* think of it?"

"I think I should kick him out of the office."

(The reader of nice perceptions, will here perceive that, it being morning, Turkey's answer is couched in polite and tranquil terms, but Nippers replies in ill-tempered ones. Or, to repeat a previous sentence, Nippers's ugly mood was on duty, and Turkey's off.)

"Ginger Nut," said I, willing to enlist the smallest suffrage in my behalf, "what do *you* think of it?"

"I think, sir, he's a little *luny*," replied Ginger Nut, with a grin.

"You hear what they say," said I, turning towards the screen, "come forth and do your duty."

But he vouchsafed no reply. I pondered a moment in sore perplexity. But once more business hurried me. I determined again to postpone the consideration of this dilemma to my future leisure. With a little trouble we made out to examine the papers without Bartleby, though at every page or two Turkey deferentially dropped his opinion, that this proceeding was quite out of the common; while Nippers, twitching in his chair with a dyspeptic nervousness, ground out, between his set teeth, occasional hissing maledictions against the stubborn oaf behind the screen. And for his (Nippers's) part, this was the first and the last time he would do another man's business without pay.

Meanwhile Bartleby sat in his hermitage, oblivious to everything but his own peculiar business there.

Some days passed, the scrivener being employed upon another lengthy work. His late remarkable conduct led me to regard his ways narrowly. I observed that he never went to dinner; indeed, that he never went anywhere. As yet I had never, of my personal knowledge, known him to be outside of my office. He was a perpetual sentry in the corner. At about eleven o'clock though, in the morning, I noticed that Ginger Nut would advance towards the opening in Bartleby's screen, as if silently beckoned thither by a gesture invisible to me where I sat. The boy would then leave the office, jingling a few pence, and reappear with a handful of ginger-nuts, which he delivered in the hermitage, receiving two of the cakes for his trouble.

He lives, then, on ginger-nuts, thought I; never eats a dinner, properly speaking; he must be a vegetarian, then; but no; he never eats even vegetables, he eats nothing but ginger-nuts. My mind then ran on in reveries concerning the probable effects upon the human constitution of living entirely on ginger-nuts. Ginger-nuts are so called, because they contain ginger as one of their peculiar constituents, and the final flavoring one. Now, what was ginger? A hot, spicy thing. Was Bartleby hot and spicy? Not at all. Ginger, then, had no effect upon Bartleby. Probably he preferred it should have none.

Nothing so aggravates an earnest person as a passive resistance. If the individual so resisted be of a not inhumane temper, and the resisting one perfectly harmless in his passivity, then, in the better moods of the former, he will endeavor charitably to construe to his imagination what proves impossible to be solved by his judgment. Even so, for the most part, I regarded Bartleby and his ways. Poor fellow! thought I, he means no mischief; it is plain he intends no insolence; his aspect sufficiently evinces that his eccentricities are involuntary. He is useful to me. I can get along with him. If I turn him away, the chances are he will fall in with some less-indulgent employer, and then he will be rudely treated, and perhaps driven forth miserably to starve. Yes. Here I can cheaply purchase a delicious self-approval. To befriend Bartleby; to humor him in his strange willfulness, will cost me little or nothing, while I lay up in my soul what will eventually prove a sweet morsel for my conscience. But this mood was not invariable with me. The passiveness of Bartleby sometimes irritated me. I felt strangely goaded on to encounter him in new opposition, to elicit some angry spark from him answerable to my own. But, indeed, I might as well have essayed to strike fire with my knuckles against a bit of Windsor soap. But one afternoon the evil impulse in me mastered me, and the following little scene ensued:

"Bartleby," said I, "when those papers are all copied, I will compare them with you."

"I would prefer not to."

"How? Surely you do not mean to persist in that mulish vagary?"

No answer.

I threw open the folding-doors near by, and, turning upon Turkey and Nippers, exclaimed:

"Bartleby a second time says, he won't examine his papers. What do you think of it, Turkey?"

It was afternoon, be it remembered. Turkey sat glowing like a brass boiler; his bald head steaming; his hands reeling among his blotted papers.

"Think of it?" roared Turkey; "I think I'll just step behind his screen, and black his eyes for him!"

So saying, Turkey rose to his feet and threw his arms into a pugilistic position. He was hurrying away to make good his promise, when I detained him, alarmed at the effect of incautiously rousing Turkey's combativeness after dinner.

"Sit down, Turkey," said I, "and hear what Nippers has to say. What do you think of it, Nippers? Would I not be justified in immediately dismissing Bartleby?"

"Excuse me, that is for you to decide, sir. I think his conduct quite unusual, and, indeed, unjust, as regards Turkey and myself. But it may only be a passing whim."

"Ah," exclaimed I, "you have strangely changed your mind, then — you speak very gently of him now."

"All beer," cried Turkey; "gentleness is effects of beer — Nippers and I dined together today. You see how gentle *I* am, sir. Shall I go and black his eyes?"

"You refer to Bartleby, I suppose. No, not today, Turkey," I replied; "pray, put up your fists."

· I closed the doors, and again advanced towards Bartleby. I felt additional incentives tempting me to my fate. I burned to be rebelled against again. I remembered that Bartleby never left the office.

"Bartleby," said I, "Ginger Nut is away; just step around to the Post Office, won't you? (it was but a three minutes' walk), and see if there is anything for me."

"I would prefer not to."

"You *will* not?"

"I *prefer* not."

I staggered to my desk, and sat there in a deep study. My blind inveteracy returned. Was there any other thing in which I could procure myself to be ignominiously re-pulsed by this lean, penniless wight? – my hired clerk? What added thing is there, perfectly reasonable, that he will be sure to refuse to do?

"Bartleby!"

No answer.

"Bartleby," in a louder tone.

No answer.

"Bartleby," I roared.

Like a very ghost, agreeably to the laws of magical invo-cation, at the third summons, he appeared at the entrance of his hermitage.

"Go to the next room, and tell Nippers to come to me."

"I prefer not to," he respectfully and slowly said, and mildly disappeared.

"Very good, Bartleby," said I, in a quiet sort of serenely-severe self-possessed tone, intimating the unalterable pur-pose of some terrible retribution very close at hand. At the moment I half intended something of the kind. But upon the whole, as it was drawing towards my dinner-hour, I thought it best to put on my hat and walk home for the day, suffering much from perplexity and distress of mind.

Shall I acknowledge it? The conclusion of this whole business was, that it soon became a fixed fact of my cham-bers, that a pale young scrivener, by the name of Bartleby, had a desk there; that he copied for me at the usual rate of four cents a folio (one hundred words); but he was perma-nently exempt from examining the work done by him, that duty being transferred to Turkey and Nippers, out of compliment, doubtless, to their superior acuteness; more-over, said Bartleby was never, on any account, to be dis-patched on the most trivial errand of any sort; and that even if entreated to take upon him such a matter, it was generally understood that he would "prefer not to" — in other words, that he would refuse point-blank.

As days passed on, I became considerably reconciled to Bartleby. His steadiness, his freedom from all dissipation, his incessant industry (except when he chose to throw himself into a standing revery behind his screen), his great stillness, his unalterableness of demeanor under all circumstances, made him a valuable acquisition. One prime thing was this — *he was always there* — first in the morning, continually through the day, and the last at night. I had a singular confidence in his honesty. I felt my most precious papers perfectly safe in his hands. Sometimes, to be sure, I could not, for the very soul of me, avoid falling into sudden spasmodic passions with him. For it was exceeding difficult to bear in mind all the time those strange peculiarities, privileges, and unheard of exemptions, forming the tacit stipulations on Bartleby's part under which he remained in my office. Now and then, in the eagerness of dispatching pressing business, I would inadvertently summon Bartleby, in a short, rapid tone, to put his finger, say, on the incipient tie of a bit of red tape with which I was about compressing some papers. Of course, from behind the screen the usual answer, "I prefer not to," was sure to come; and then, how could a human creature, with the common infirmities of our nature, refrain from bitterly exclaiming upon such perverseness — such unreasonableness. However, every added repulse of this sort which I received only tended to lessen the probability of my repeating the inadvertence.

On Idleness
MICHEL DE MONTAIGNE, 1572-73

The French essayist Montaigne was particularly in love with sleep — so much so that he used to get people to wake him in order that he might catch a glimpse of this glorious state. Here we find him in typically self-deprecatory form.

*A*s we see ground that lies fallow, teeming, if rich and fertile, with countless kinds of wild and useless plants, and observe that, to keep it serviceable, we must master it and sow it with various crops of use to ourselves; and as we see that women, of themselves, sometimes bring forth inanimate and shapeless lumps of flesh, but to produce a sound and natural birth must be fertilized with different seed, so it is with our minds. If we do not occupy them with some definite subject which curbs and restrains them, they rush wildly to and fro in the ill-defined field of the imagination,

> *Sicut aquae tremulum labris ubi lumen abenis*
> *sole repercussum, aut radiantis imagine Lunae*
> *omnia pervolitat late loca, iamque sub auras*
> *erigitur, summique ferit laquearia tecti.*

[As water, trembling in a brass bowl, reflects the sun's light or the form of the shining moon, and so the bright beams flit in all directions, darting up at times to strike the lofty fretted ceilings. Virgil, *Aeneid*, vii, 22.]

And there is no folly or fantasy that they will not produce in this restless state.

velut aegri somnia, vanae finguntur species.

[Unreal monsters are imagined, like a sick man's dreams. Horace, *Ars Poetica*, 7.]

The mind that has no fixed aim loses itself, for, as they say, to be everywhere is to be nowhere.

Quisquis ubique habitat, Maxime, nusquam habitat.

[A man who lives everywhere, Maximus, lives nowhere. Martial, vii, 73.]

When lately I retired to my house resolved that, in so far as I could, I would cease – to concern myself with anything except the passing in rest and retirement of the little time I still have to live, I could do my mind no better service than to leave it in complete idleness to commune with itself, to come to rest, and to grow settled; which I hoped it would thenceforth be able to do more easily, since it had become graver and more mature with time. But I find,

> *variam semper dant otia mentem.* [Leisure always breeds an inconstant mind. Lucan, iv, 704.]

that, on the contrary, like a runaway horse, it is a hundred times more active on its own behalf than ever it was for others. It presents me with so many chimeras and imaginary monsters, one after another, without order or plan, that, in order to contemplate their oddness and absurdity at leisure, I have begun to record them in writing, hoping in time to make my mind ashamed of them.

---

from *Phrases and Philosophies for the Use of the Young*
OSCAR WILDE, 1894

*T*he condition of perfection is idleness; the aim of perfection is youth.

An Apology for Idlers
ROBERT LOUIS STEVENSON, 1876

In this spirited defense of the lazy life, a 26-year-old Robert Louis Stevenson argues that to be idle is a sign of inner confidence.

BOSWELL: We grow weary when idle.

JOHNSON: That is, sir, because others being busy, we want company; but if we were idle, there would be no growing weary; we should all entertain one another.

Just now, when everyone is bound, under pain of a decree in absence convicting them of *lèse*-respectability, to enter on some lucrative profession, and labor therein with something not far short of enthusiasm, a cry from the opposite party who are content when they have enough, and like to look on and enjoy in the meanwhile, savors a little of bravado and gasconade. And yet this should not be. Idleness so called, which does not consist in doing nothing, but in doing a great deal not recognized in the dogmatic formularies of the ruling class, has as good a right to state its position as industry itself. It is admitted that the presence of people who refuse to enter in the great handicap race for six-penny pieces, is at once an insult and a disenchantment for those who do. A fine fellow (as we see so many) takes his determination, votes for the sixpences, and in the emphatic Americanism, "goes for" them. And while such a one is ploughing distressfully up the road, it is not hard to understand his resentment, when he perceives cool persons in the meadows by the wayside, lying with a handkerchief over their ears and a glass at their elbow. Alexander is touched in a very delicate place by the disregard of Diogenes. Where was the glory of having taken Rome for these tumultuous barbarians, who poured into the Senate house, and found the Fathers sitting silent and unmoved by their success? It is a sore thing to have labored along and scaled the arduous hilltops, and when all is done, find humanity indifferent to your achievement. Hence physicists condemn the unphysical; financiers have only a superficial toleration for those who know little of stocks; literary persons despise the unlettered; and people of all pursuits combine to disparage those who have none.

But though this is one difficulty of the subject, it is not the greatest. You could not be put in prison for speaking against industry, but you can be sent to Coventry for speaking like a fool. The greatest difficulty with most subjects is to do them well; therefore, please to remember this is an apology. It is certain that much may be judiciously argued in favor of diligence; only there is something to be said against it, and that is what, on the present occasion, I have to say. To state one argument is not necessarily to be deaf to all others, and that a man has written a book of travels in Montenegro, is no reason why he should never have been to Richmond.

It is surely beyond a doubt that people should be a good deal idle in youth. For though here and there a Lord Macaulay may escape from school honors with all his wits about him, most boys pay so dear for their medals that they never afterwards have a shot in their locker, and begin the world bankrupt. And the same holds true during all the time a lad is educating himself, or suffering others to educate him. It must have been a very foolish old gentleman who addressed Johnson at Oxford in these words: "Young man, ply your book diligently now, and acquire a stock of knowledge; for when years come upon you, you will find that poring upon books will be but an irksome task." The old gentleman seems to have been unaware that many other things besides reading grow irksome, and not a few become impossible, by the time a man has to use spectacles and cannot walk without a stick. Books are good enough in their own way, but they are a mighty bloodless substitute for life. It seems a pity to sit, like the Lady of Shalott, peering into a mirror, with your back turned on all the bustle and glamour of reality. And if a man reads very hard, as the old anecdote reminds us, he will have little time for thought.

If you look back on your own education, I am sure it will not be the full, vivid, instructive hours of truantry that you regret; you would rather cancel some lack-luster periods between sleep and waking in the class. For my own part, I have attended a good many lectures in my time. I still remember that the spinning of a top is a case of Kinetic Stability. I still remember that Emphyteusis is not a disease, nor Stillicide a crime. But though I would not willingly part with such scraps of science, I do not set the same store by them as by certain other odds and ends that I came by in the open street while I was playing truant. This is not the moment to dilate on that mighty place of education, which was the favorite school of Dickens and of Balzac, and turns out yearly many inglorious masters in the Science of the Aspects of Life. Suffice it to say this: if a lad does not learn in the streets, it is because he has no faculty of learning. Nor is the truant always in the streets, for if he prefers, he may go out by the gardened suburbs into the country. He may pitch on some tuft of lilacs over a burn, and smoke innumerable pipes to the tune of the water on the stones. A bird will sing in the thicket. And there he may fall into a vein of kindly thought, and see things in a new perspective. Why, if this be not education, what is? We may conceive Mr. Worldly Wiseman accosting such an one, and the conversation that should thereupon ensue: —

"How now, young fellow, what dost thou here?"

"Truly, sir, I take mine ease."

"Is not this the hour of the class? and should'st thou not be plying thy Book with diligence, to the end thou mayest obtain knowledge?"

"Nay, but thus also I follow after Learning, by your leave."

"Learning, quotha! After what fashion, I pray thee? Is it mathematics?"

"No, to be sure."

"Is it metaphysics?"

"Nor that."

"Is it some language?"

"Nay, it is no language."

"Is it a trade?"

"Nor a trade neither."

"Why, then, what is't?"

"Indeed, sir, as a time may soon come for me to go upon Pilgrimage, I am desirous to note what is commonly done by persons in my case, and where are the ugliest Sloughs and Thickets on the Road; as also, what manner of Staff is of the best service. Moreover, I lie here, by this water, to learn by root-of-heart a lesson which my master teaches me to call Peace, or Contentment."

Hereupon Mr. Worldly Wiseman was much commoved with passion, and shaking his cane with a very threatful countenance, broke forth upon this wise: "Learning, quotha!" said he; "I would have all such rogues scourged by the Hangman!"

And so he would go his way, ruffling out his cravat with a crackle of starch, like a turkey when it spread its feathers.

Now this, of Mr. Wiseman's, is the common opinion. A fact is not called a fact, but a piece of gossip, if it does not fall into one of your scholastic categories. An inquiry must be in some acknowledged direction, with a name to go by; or else you are not inquiring at all, only lounging; and the workhouse is too good for you. It is supposed that all knowledge is at the bottom of a well, or the far end of a telescope. Sainte-Beuve, as he grew older, came to regard all experience as a single great book, in which to study for a few years ere we go hence; and it seemed all one to him whether you should read in Chapter xx, which is the differential calculus, or in Chapter xxxix, which is hearing the band play in the gardens. As a matter of fact, an intelligent person, looking out of his eyes and hearkening in his ears, with a smile on his face all the time, will get more true education than many another in a life of heroic vigils. There is certainly some chill and arid knowledge to be found upon the summits of formal and laborious science; but it is all round about you, and for the trouble of looking, that you will acquire the warm and palpitating facts of life. While others are filling their memory with a lumber of words, one-half of which they will forget before the week be out, your truant may learn some really useful art: to play the fiddle, to know a good cigar, or to speak with ease and opportunity to all varieties of men. Many who have "plied their book diligently," and know all about some one branch or another of accepted lore, come out of the study with an ancient and owl-like demeanor, and prove dry, stockish, and dyspeptic in all the better and brighter parts of life. Many make a large fortune, who remain underbred and pathetically stupid to the last. And meantime there goes the idler, who began life along with them — by your leave, a different picture. He has had time to take care of his health and his spirits; he has been a great deal in the open air, which is the most salutary of all things for both body and mind; and if he has never read the great Book in very recondite places, he has dipped into it and skimmed it over to excellent purpose. Might not the student afford some Hebrew roots, and the business man some of his half-crowns, for a share of the idler's knowledge of life at large, and Art of Living? Nay, and the idler has another and more important quality than these. I mean his wisdom. He who has much looked on at the childish satisfaction of other people in their hobbies, will regard his own with only a very ironical indulgence. He will not be heard among the dogmatists. He will have a great and cool allowance for all sorts of people and opinions. If he finds no out-of-the-way truths, he will identify himself with no very burning false-hood. His way takes him along a by-road, not much fre-quented, but very even and pleasant, which is called Commonplace Lane, and leads to the Belvedere of Com-monsense. Thence he shall command an agreeable, if no very noble prospect; and while others behold the East and West, the Devil and the Sunrise, he will be contentedly aware of a sort of morning hour upon all sublunary things, with an army of shadows running speedily and in many different directions into the great daylight of Eternity. The shadows and the generations, the shrill doctors and the plangent wars, go by into ultimate silence and emptiness; but underneath all this, a man may see, out of the Belvedere windows, much green and peaceful landscape; many firelit parlors; good people laughing, drinking, and making love as they did before the Flood or the French Revolution; and the old shepherd telling his tale under the hawthorn.

Extreme *busyness*, whether at school or college, kirk or market, is a symptom of deficient vitality; and a faculty for idleness implies a catholic appetite and a strong sense of personal identity. There is a sort of dead-alive, hackneyed people about, who are scarcely conscious of living except in the exercise of some conventional occupation. Bring these fellows into the country, or set them aboard ship, and you will see how they pine for their desk or their study. They have no curiosity; they cannot give themselves over to random provocations; they do not take pleasure in the exercise of their faculties for its own sake; and unless Necessity lays about them with a stick, they will even stand still. It is no good speaking to such folk: they *cannot* be idle, their nature is not generous enough; and they pass those hours in a sort of coma, which are not dedicated to furious moiling in the goldmill. When they do not require to go to the office, when they are not hungry and have no mind to drink, the whole breathing world is a blank to them. If they have to wait an hour or so for a train, they fall into a stupid trance with their eyes open. To see them, you would suppose there was nothing to look at and no one to speak with; you would imagine they were paralyzed or alienated; and yet very possibly they are hard workers in their own way, and have good eyesight for a flaw in a deed or a turn of the market. They have been to school and college, but all the time they had their eye on the medal; they have gone about in the world and mixed with clever people, but all the time they were thinking of their own affairs. As if a man's soul were not too small to begin with, they have dwarfed and narrowed theirs by a life of all work and no play; until here they are at forty, with a listless attention, a mind vacant of all material of amusement, and not one thought to rub against another, while they wait for the train. Before he was breeched, he might have clambered on the boxes; when he was twenty, he would have stared at the girls; but now the pipe is smoked out, the snuff-box empty, and my gentleman sits bolt upright upon a bench, with lamentable eyes. This does not appeal to me as being Success in Life.

But it is not only the person himself who suffers from his busy habits, but his wife and children, his friends and relations, and down to the very people he sits with in a railway carriage or an omnibus. Perpetual devotion to what a man calls his business, is only to be sustained by perpetual neglect of many other things. And it is not by any means certain that a man's business is the most important thing he has to do. To an impartial estimate it will seem clear that many of the wisest, most virtuous, and most beneficent parts that are to be played upon the Theater of Life are filled by gratuitous performers, and pass, among the world at large, as phases of idleness. For in that Theater, not only the walking gentlemen, singing chambermaids, and diligent fiddlers in the orchestra, but those who look on and clap their hands from the benches, do really play a part and fulfill important offices towards the general result. You are no doubt very dependent on the care of your lawyer and stockbroker, of the guards and signalmen who convey you rapidly from place to place, and the policemen who walk the streets for your protection; but is there not a thought of gratitude in your heart for certain other benefactors who set you smiling when they fall in your way, or season your dinner with good company? Colonel Newcome helped to lose his friend's money; Fred Bayham had an ugly trick of borrowing shirts; and yet they were better people to fall among than Mr. Barnes. And though Falstaff was neither sober nor very honest, I think I could name one or two long-faced Barabbases whom the world could better have done without. Hazlitt mentions that he was more sensible of obligation to Northcote, who had never done him anything he could call a service, than to his whole circle of ostentatious friends; for he thought a good companion emphatically the greatest benefactor. I know there are people in the world who cannot feel grateful unless the favor has been done them at the cost of pain and difficulty. But this is a churlish disposition. A man may send you six sheets of letter-paper covered with the most entertaining gossip, or you may pass half an hour pleasantly, perhaps profitably, over an article of his; do you think the service would be greater, if he had made the manuscript in his heart's blood, like a compact with the devil? Do you really fancy you should be more beholden to your correspondent, if he had been damning you all the while for your importunity? Pleasures are more beneficial than duties because, like the quality of mercy, they are not strained, and they are twice blest. There must always be two to a kiss, and there may be a score in a jest; but wherever there is an element of sacrifice, the favor is conferred with pain, and, among generous people, received with confusion. There is no duty we so much underrate as the duty of being happy. By being happy, we sow anonymous benefits upon the world, which remain unknown even to ourselves, or when they are disclosed, surprise nobody so much as the benefactor. The other day, a ragged, barefoot boy ran down the street after a marble, with so jolly an air that he set every one he passed into a good humor; one of these persons, who had been delivered from more than usually black thoughts, stopped the little fellow and gave him some money with this remark: "You see what sometimes comes of looking pleased." If he had looked pleased before, he had now to look both pleased and mystified. For my part, I justify this encouragement of smiling rather than tearful children; I do not wish to pay for tears anywhere but upon the stage; but I am prepared to deal largely in the opposite commodity. A happy man or woman is a better thing to find than a five-pound note. He or she is a radiating focus of goodwill; and their entrance into a room is as though another candle had been lighted. We need not care whether they could prove the forty-seventh proposition; they do a better thing than that, they practically demonstrate the great Theorem of the Livableness of Life. Consequently, if a person cannot be happy without remaining idle, idle he should remain. It is a revolutionary precept; but thanks to hunger and the workhouse, one not easily to be abused; and within practical limits, it is one of the most incontestable truths in the whole Body of Morality. Look at one of your industrious fellows for a moment, I beseech you. He sows hurry and reaps indigestion; he puts a vast deal of activity out to interest, and receives a large measure of nervous derangement in return. Either he absents himself entirely from all fellowship, and lives a recluse in a garret, with carpet slippers and a leaden inkpot; or he comes among people swiftly and bitterly, in a contraction of his whole nervous system, to discharge some temper before he returns to work. I do not care how much or how well he works, this fellow is an evil feature in other people's lives. They would be happier if he were dead. They could easier do without his services in the Circumlocution Office, than they can tolerate his fractious spirits. He poisons life at the wellhead. It is better to be beggared out of hand by a scapegrace nephew, than daily hagridden by a peevish uncle.

And what, in God's name, is all this pother about? For what cause do they embitter their own and other people's lives? That a man should publish three or thirty articles a year, that he should finish or not finish his great allegorical picture, are questions of little interest to the world. The ranks of life are full; and although a thousand fall, there are always some to go into the breach. When they told Joan of Arc she should be at home minding women's work, she answered there were plenty to spin and wash. And so, even with your own rare gifts! When nature is "so careless of the single life," why should we coddle ourselves into the fancy that our own is of exceptional importance? Suppose Shakespeare had been knocked on the head some dark night in Sir Thomas Lucy's preserves, the world would have wagged on better or worse, the pitcher gone to the well, the scythe to the corn, and the student to his book; and no one been any the wiser of the loss. There are not many works extant, if you look the alternative all over, which are worth the price of a pound of tobacco to a man of limited means. This is a sobering reflection for the proudest of our earthly vanities. Even a tobacconist may, upon consideration, find no great cause for personal vainglory in the phrase; for although tobacco is an admirable sedative, the qualities necessary for retailing it are neither rare nor precious in themselves. Alas and alas! you may take it how you will, but the services of no single individual are indispensable. Atlas was just a gentleman with a protracted nightmare! And yet you see merchants who go and labor themselves into a great fortune and thence into the bankruptcy court; scribblers who keep scribbling at little articles until their temper is a cross to all who come about them, as though Pharaoh should set the Israelites to make a pin instead of a pyramid; and fine young men who work themselves into a decline, and are driven off in a hearse with white plumes upon it. Would you not suppose these persons had been whispered, by the Master of the Ceremonies, the promise of some momentous destiny? and that this lukewarm bullet on which they play their farces was the bull's-eye and centerpoint of all the universe? And yet it is not so. The ends for which they give away their priceless youth, for all they know, may be chimerical or hurtful; the glory and riches they expect may never come, or may find them indifferent; and they and the world they inhabit are so inconsiderable that the mind freezes at the thought.

The Idler, No. 30

SAMUEL JOHNSON, 1758

In which Dr. Johnson rails against the news-writers of his day, who, in his view, provided tittle-tattle for those with nothing else to do.

The desires of man increase with his acquisitions; every step which he advances brings something within his view, which he did not see before, and which, as soon as he sees it, he begins to want. Where necessity ends curiosity begins, and no sooner are we supplied with every thing that nature can demand, than we sit down to contrive artificial appetites.

By this restlessness of mind, every populous and wealthy city is filled with innumerable employments, for which the greater part of mankind is without a name; with artificers whose labor is exerted in producing such petty conveniences, that many shops are furnished with instruments, of which the use can hardly be found without inquiry, but which he that once knows them, quickly learns to number among necessary things.

Such is the diligence, with which, in countries completely civilized, one part of mankind labors for another, that wants are supplied faster than they can be formed, and the idle and luxurious find life stagnate, for want of some desire to keep it in motion. This species of distress furnishes a new set of occupations, and multitudes are busied, from day to day, in finding the rich and the fortunate something to do.

It is very common to reproach those artists as useless, who produce only such superfluities as neither accommodate the body nor improve the mind; and of which no other effect can be imagined, than that they are the occasions of spending money, and consuming time.

But this censure will be mitigated, when it is seriously considered, that money and time are the heaviest burdens of life, and that the unhappiest of all mortals are those who have more of either than they know how to use. To set himself free from these encumbrances, one hurries to Newmarket; another travels over Europe; one pulls down his house and calls architects about him; another buys a seat in the country, and follows his hounds over hedges and through rivers; one makes collections of shells, and another searches the world for tulips and carnations.

He is surely a public benefactor who finds employment for those to whom it is thus difficult to find it for themselves. It is true that this is seldom done merely from generosity or compassion, almost every man seeks his own advantage in helping others, and therefore it is too common for mercenary officiousness, to consider rather what is grateful than what is right.

We all know that it is more profitable to be loved than esteemed, and ministers of pleasure will always be found, who study to make themselves necessary, and to supplant those who are practicing the same arts.

One of the amusements of idleness is reading without the fatigue of close attention, and the world therefore swarms with writers whose wish is not to be studied but to be read.

No species of literary men has lately been so much multiplied as the writers of news. Not many years ago the nation was content with one *Gazette*; but now we have not only in the metropolis papers for every morning and every evening, but almost every large town has its weekly historian, who regularly circulates his periodical intelligence, and fills the villages of his district with conjectures on the events of war, and with debates on the true interest of Europe.

To write news in its perfection requires such a combination of qualities, that a man completely fitted for the task is not always to be found. In Sir Henry Wotton's jocular definition, "An ambassador" is said to be "a man of virtue sent abroad to tell lies for the advantage of his country"; a news-writer is "a man without virtue, who writes lies at home for his own profit." To these compositions is required neither genius nor knowledge, neither industry nor sprightliness, but contempt of shame and indifference to truth are absolutely necessary. He who by a long familiarity with infamy has obtained these qualities, may confidently tell today what he intends to contradict tomorrow; he may affirm fearlessly what he knows that he shall be obliged to recant, and may write letters from Amsterdam or Dresden to himself.

In a time of war the nation is always of one mind, eager to hear something good of themselves and ill of the enemy. At this time the task of news-writers is easy, they have nothing to do but to tell that a battle is expected, and afterwards that a battle has been fought, in which we and our friends, whether conquering or conquered, did all, and our enemies did nothing.

Scarce any thing awakens attention like a tale of cruelty. The writer of news never fails in the intermission of action to tell how the enemies murdered children and ravished virgins; and if the scene of action be somewhat distant, scalps half the inhabitants of a province.

Among the calamities of war may be justly numbered the diminution of the love of truth, by the falsehoods which interest dictates and credulity encourages. A peace will equally leave the warrior and relator of wars destitute of employment; and I know not whether more is to be dreaded from streets filled with soldiers accustomed to plunder, or from garrets filled with scribblers accustomed to lie.

from *Oblomov*

IVAN GONCHAROV, 1859

Here Oblomov's sublime lassitude is described, for the comfort and entertainment of us all.

Oblomov, a gentleman by birth and a collegiate secretary by rank, had lived for the last twelve years in Petersburg.

At first, while his parents were still living, he had a lodging of two rooms only and was content with the services of Zahar, whom he had brought with him from the country. But when his father and mother died he became the sole owner of three hundred and fifty serfs, inherited by him in one of the distant provinces near the borders of Asia. Instead of five he now received from seven to ten thousand paper rubles a year, and his style of living expanded accordingly. He took a bigger flat, hired a chef, and kept a pair of horses. He was young then, and though one could not say he was lively, he was at any rate more alive than now; he was still full of plans, still hoped for something, expected a great deal both from fate and from himself; he was eager to achieve something, to play his part – in the first instance, of course, in the service for the sake of which he had come to Petersburg. He thought, too, of playing a part in society; and in the distant future, at the turning-point between youth and maturity, family happiness flitted brightly before his imagination. But days and years passed by: the soft down on his chin turned into stiff bristles, his shining eyes became dimmed, his waist broadened, his hair had begun to come out cruelly, he was turned thirty, and he had not advanced a step in any direction and was still standing at the threshold of his career as ten years before.

Life was divided, in his opinion, into two halves: one consisted of work and boredom — these words were for him synonymous — the other of rest and peaceful good-humor. This was the reason why his chief field of activity — Government service — proved to be an unpleasant surprise to him at the very outset.

Brought up in the depths of the country amidst the gentle and kindly manners and customs of his native province, he spent the first twenty years of his life in the embraces of his relatives, friends, and acquaintances, and was so permeated with the family principle that his future service appeared to him as a sort of family pursuit, such, for instance, as lazily putting down income and expenditure in a notebook, as his father had done. He imagined that the officials in the same Department were one friendly, closely knit family, unwearyingly striving for one another's peace and pleasure; that going daily to the office was by no means compulsory, and that bad weather, heat, or mere disinclination were sufficient and legitimate reasons for missing a day. How grieved he was when he saw nothing short of an earthquake could prevent an official in good health from going to his work — and unfortunately earthquakes never happened in Petersburg! A flood might, of course, also be regarded as an obstacle, but even floods happened rarely. Oblomov felt still more troubled when envelopes inscribed "important" and "very important" flitted before his eyes, and he was asked to make various inquiries and quotations, to look through papers, to write folios two inches thick, which were called, as though in mockery, "notes." To make matters worse, everything had to be done in a hurry — everyone seemed to rush and never to rest; they had no sooner finished one case than they furiously seized upon another, as though it were the one that mattered, and when they had done with that they forgot it and pounced upon a third — and there was no end to it! Twice he had been roused at night and made to write "notes," several times he had been fetched by a courier from a visit to friends — always because of those notes. All this frightened him and bored him terribly. "But when am I to live?" he repeated in distress.

He had heard at home, in the country, that a superior officer was a father to his subordinates and had formed a most cheering and homely idea of such a person. He imagined him as a kind of fond parent whose only concern was constantly to reward his subordinates whether they deserved it or no, and to provide both for their needs and for their pleasures. Ilya Ilyitch had thought that a superior was so concerned with his subordinate's welfare that he would carefully ask him how he had slept, why his eyes looked dim, and whether his head ached. But he was bitterly disappointed on his very first day at the office. When the chief arrived there was a great deal of fuss, scurry, and confusion: the officials ran into one another, some began to pull their uniforms straight, for fear they were not tidy enough to appear before him. As Oblomov observed afterwards, all this commotion was due to the fact that some chiefs read in the stupidly frightened faces of their subordinates rushing out to meet them not only respect for themselves but zeal for the service, and sometimes even ability for it. Ilya Ilyitch had no need to be afraid of his chief, a kind and pleasant man, who had never done any harm to anyone; his subordinates were highly satisfied and wished for nothing better. No one had ever heard an unpleasant word from him; he never shouted or made an uproar, never re-

quested but always asked. He asked, whether it was a case
of work, or of paying him a call, or of being put under ar-
rest. He had never been rude to his subordinates either in-
dividually or collectively; but somehow they were timid in
his presence; they answered his kind questions in an un-
natural voice, such as they never used in speaking to other
people. And Ilya Ilyitch, too, was suddenly afraid, without
knowing why, when the chief came into the room, and he,
too, began to lose his ordinary voice and to speak in an abject falsetto as soon as the chief addressed him.

Ilya Ilyitch was worn out with fear and misery serving
under a kind and easy-going chief; Heaven only knows
what would have become of him had he had a stern and
exacting one! Oblomov managed to stay in the service for
two years; he might have endured it for a third and obtained a rank had not a special incident caused him to re-
sign. He once sent an important paper to Archangel
instead of to Astrakhan. This was found out; a search was
made for the culprit. All the others were waiting with interest for the chief to call Oblomov and ask him coldly and
deliberately "whether he had sent the paper to Archangel," and everyone wondered in what sort of voice Ilya Ilyitch would reply. Some thought he would not reply at all —
would not be able to. The general atmosphere infected Ilya
Ilyitch; he was frightened, too, although he knew that the
chief would do nothing worse than reprimand him. His
own conscience, however, was much sterner than any reprimand; he did not wait for the punishment he deserved,
but went home and sent in a medical certificate.

The certificate was as follows: "I, the undersigned, certify
and append my seal thereto that the collegiate secretary,
Ilya Oblomov, suffers from an enlarged heart and a dilation

of its left ventricle *(Hypertrophia cordis cum dilatione ejus ventriculi sinistri)*, and also from a chronic pain in the liver *(hepatitis)*, which may endanger the patient's health and life, the attacks being due, it is to be surmised, to his going daily to the office. Therefore, to prevent the repetition and increase of these painful attacks, I find it necessary to forbid Mr. Oblomov to go to the office and insist that he should altogether abstain from intellectual pursuits and any sort of activity."

But this helped for a time only: sooner or later he had to recover and then there was the prospect of daily going to the office again. Oblomov could not endure it and sent in his resignation. So ended, never to be resumed again, his work for the State.

His social career was at first more successful. During his early years in Petersburg his placid features were more frequently animated; his eyes often glowed with the fire of life and shone with light, hope, energy. He was stirred to excitement like other people, hoped and rejoiced at trifles, and suffered from trifles too. But that was long ago, at that tender age when one regards every man as a sincere friend, falls in love with almost every woman, and is ready to offer her one's hand and heart — which some, indeed, succeed in doing, often to their profound regret for the rest of their lives. In those blissful days Ilya Ilyitch, too, had received not a few tender, soft, and even passionate glances from the crowd of beauties, a number of promising smiles, two or three stolen kisses, and many friendly handclasps that hurt to tears.

He was never held captive by the beauties, however, never was their slave or even a very assiduous admirer, if only because intimacy with a woman involves a lot of exertion. For the most part, Oblomov confined himself to admiring them from a respectful distance. Very seldom did fate throw him so much together with a woman that he could catch fire for a few days and believe that he was in love. His sentimental feelings never developed into love affairs; they stopped short at the very beginning, and were as innocent, pure, and simple as the loves of a schoolgirl.

He particularly avoided the pale, melancholy maidens, generally with black eyes reflecting "bitter days and sinful nights"; hollow-eyed maidens with mysterious joys and sorrows, who always want to confide in their friend, to tell him something, and, when it comes to telling, shudder, burst into tears, throw their arms round his neck, gaze into his eyes, then at the sky, say that the curse of destiny is upon them, and sometimes fall down in a faint. Oblomov feared them and kept away. His soul was still pure and virginal; it may have been waiting for the right moment, for real love, for ecstatic passion, and then with years it seemed to have despaired of waiting.

Ilya Ilyitch parted still more coldly with the crowd of his friends. After the first letter from his bailiff about arrears and failure of crops, he replaced his chief friend, the chef, by a female cook, then sold his horses, and at last dismissed his other "friends."

Hardly any outside attractions existed for him, and every day he grew more firmly rooted in his flat.

At first he found it irksome to remain dressed all day, then he felt lazy about dining out except with intimate bachelor friends, at whose houses he could take off his tie, unbutton his waistcoat, and even lie down and have an hour's sleep. Evening-parties soon wearied him also: one had to put on a dress-coat, to shave every day. Having read somewhere that only the morning dew was good for one and the evening dew was bad, he began to fear the damp. In

spite of all these fancies his friend Stolz succeeded in making him go and see people; but Stolz often left Petersburg
for Moscow, Nizhni, the Crimea, and foreign parts, and
without him Oblomov again wholly abandoned himself to
solitude and seclusion that could only be disturbed by
something unusual, out of the ordinary routine of life; but
nothing of the sort happened or was likely to happen.

Besides, as Oblomov grew older he reverted to a kind of
childish timidity, expecting harm and danger from everything that was beyond the range of his everyday life — the
result of losing touch with external events.

He was not afraid of the crack in his bedroom ceiling —
he was used to it; it did not occur to him that stuffy atmosphere and perpetual sitting indoors might be more peril-
ous for his health than night dampness, or that continual
overfeeding was a kind of slow suicide; he was used to it
and was not afraid. He was not used to movement, to life,
to seeing many people, to bustling about. He felt stifled in a
dense crowd; he stepped into a boat feeling uncertain of
reaching the other bank; he drove in a carriage expecting
the horses to bolt and smash it. Sometimes he had an attack of purely nervous fear: he was afraid of the stillness
around him or he did not know himself of what — a cold
shiver ran down his body. He nervously peeped at a dark
corner, expecting his imagination to trick him into seeing
some supernatural apparition.

This was the end to which his social life had come. With
a lazy wave of his hand he dismissed all the youthful hopes
that had betrayed him or been betrayed by him, all the tender, melancholy, and bright memories that make some
people's hearts beat faster even in their old age.

from *On Presumption*

MICHEL DE MONTAIGNE, 1580

*S*kill and agility were never mine; and yet I am the son of a very active father, who remained agile into extreme old age. He could hardly find a man in his station who was his equal in all physical exercises, while I have seldom met anyone who did not excel me in any but running, at which I was moderately good. In music, either for the voice – for which mine is very ill-suited – or instrumental, they were never able to teach me anything. In dancing, tennis, or wrestling, I was never able to acquire more than a very slight and ordinary competence; in swimming, fencing, vaulting, and leaping, none at all. My hands are so awkward that what I write is illegible even to me; and so, when I have scribbled something down I would rather work it all out again than give myself the trouble of deciphering it. And I do not read much better. I feel that I weary my hearers. Otherwise, a fair scholar. I cannot fold a letter properly, and have never been able to cut a pen, or carve well at table, or saddle and bridle a horse, or carry a hawk on my fist and cast her off, or control dogs, birds, or horses.

In short, my physical qualities are much on a par with those of my mind. There is nothing sprightly about them; there is only a full, firm vigor. I can stand hard work, but only when it is voluntary, and for so long as my desire prompts me.

Molliter austerum studio fallente laborem.

[With eagerness deceptively lightening hard work.
Horace, *Satires*, ii, ii. 12.]

Otherwise, unless I am allured to it by some pleasure, and have no other guide than pure free will, I am of no use at all. For I have come to the point where there is nothing I will bite my nails over except life and health, nothing that I am willing to purchase at the price of mental torment and constraint,

> *tanti mihi non sint opaci*
> *omnis arena Tagi, quodque in mare volvitur aurum.*

> [I would not buy all Tagus's dark sands at such a price, not all the gold it washes into the sea. Juvenal, III, 54 (adapted).]

I am extremely idle and extremely independent both by nature and by intention. I would as willingly lend my blood as my pains.

I have a mind that belongs wholly to itself, and is accustomed to go its own way. Having never until this hour had a master or governor imposed on me, I have advanced as far as I pleased, and at my own pace. This has made me slack and unfit for the service of others; it has made me useless to any but myself.

And, in my own interest, there has been no need to put pressure on this heavy, indolent, and inactive nature. For having enjoyed from birth such a degree of fortune that I have had reason to be content with it, and as much intelligence as I have felt I had occasion for, I have sought for nothing and taken nothing:

> *Non agimur tumidis velis Aquilone secundo;*
> *non tamen adversis aetatem ducimus austris:*
> *viribus, ingenio, specie, virtute, loco, re,*
> *extremi primorum, extremis usque priores.*

[My sails are not filled by the favoring north winds nor is
my voyage troubled by the hostile south winds. In
strength, intelligence, looks, in virtue, place, and possessions, although the last of the great, I am among the first
of the last. Horace, *Epistles*, ii, ii, 201.]

It has taken only a sufficiency to content me. But this
implies, if properly understood, a disciplined mind, which
is hard to attain in any walk of life, and which, in practice,
we find to exist more easily with want than with abundance; since, as with our other passions, the appetite for
riches is perhaps made sharper by their enjoyment than by
their scarcity, and the virtue of moderation is rarer than
that of patience. All that I have needed has been quietly to
enjoy the good things that God, in His bounty, has put into
my hands.

I have never had a taste for any sort of tiresome labor. I
have hardly ever managed any business but my own; or if I
have, it has been on condition that I did things in my own
time and in my own way. And I have only acted for people
who trusted me, and did not bother me, and knew me
well. For expert riders will get some service even from a
restive and broken-winded horse.

Even my childish upbringing was gentle and free, and
subject to no rigorous discipline. All this bred in me a sensitive disposition, incapable of bearing worries; to such a
degree that I like to have any losses or troubles that concern me concealed from my knowledge. I enter under the
head of expenses the sum that it costs me to keep my neg-
ligence fed and maintained.

haec nempe supersunt,
quae dominum fallant, quae prosint furibus.

[These are superfluities, that slip from the master's hands
for the profit of thieves. Horace, *Epistles* I, vi, 45.]

I prefer to have no inventory of my possessions, so that I
may be the less sensible of a loss. I beg those who live with
me, if they lack affection and honesty, at least to pay me
the tribute of outward decency when they cheat me. Since
I have not the steadfastness to bear the annoyance of those
unfortunate accidents to which we are subject, and cannot
endure the strain of regulating and managing my affairs, I
leave myself entirely in fortune's hands, encouraging myself, to the best of my ability, to the idea that everything
will be for the worst, and resolving to bear that worst with
meekness and patience. For this alone do I strive; it is the
aim to which I direct all my thoughts.

When in danger, I do not consider so much how I shall
escape as how little it matters whether I escape or not. If I
were to succumb to it, what would that amount to? Not
being able to control events, I control myself, and adapt
myself to them if they do not adapt themselves to me. I
have hardly the skill to circumvent fortune, or to escape
and overcome it, or wisely to arrange and incline things to
serve my purpose. Still less have I the patience to resist the
sharp and painful anxieties that such action entails. And
the most painful situation for me is to be in suspense about
urgent matters, and tossed between fear and hope.

Deliberation, even in the most trivial affairs, is irksome
to me; and my mind is more put about when suffering the
shocks and trepidations of uncertainty and doubt than in
settling down and accepting whatever happens, once the
die is cast. My sleep has been broken by few passions; but
the slightest suspense will break it. When travelling, I pre-

fer to avoid steep and slippery slopes, and to follow the beaten track, however deep the mud, for though I may sink in, that is the lowest I can fall, and I choose it as a measure of safety. Similarly, I prefer a disaster unalloyed, in which I am no longer tormented by the possibility that things may improve. I prefer to be plunged straight into suffering at the first blow,

> *dubia plus torquent mala*

> [Uncertain evils torture us more. Seneca, *Agamemnon*, III, i, 29.]

When the thing has happened I behave like a man; when I have to manage it, like a child. Fear of a fall makes me more feverish than the fall itself. The game is not worth the candle. A miser suffers worse from his passion than a poor man, a jealous man than a cuckold. And often there is less harm in losing one's vineyard than in going to law for it. The lowest step is the firmest. It is the seat of constancy. There you have need of no one but yourself. It has its own foundation, and rests solely on itself.

On Lying in Bed

G.K. CHESTERTON, 1926

Best known for his Father Brown novels, Chesterton also had a fine appreciation of the true location of inspiration: the bed.

Lying in bed would be an altogether perfect and supreme experience if only one had a colored pencil long enough to draw on the ceiling. This, however, is not generally a part of the domestic apparatus on the premises. I think myself that the thing might be managed with several pails of Aspinall and a broom. Only if one worked in a really sweeping and masterly way, and laid on the colors in great washes, it might drop down again on one's face in floods of rich and mingled color like some strange fairy rain; and that would have its disadvantages. I am afraid it would be necessary to stick to black and white in this form of artistic composition. To that purpose, indeed, the white ceiling would be of the greatest possible use; in fact it is the only use I think of a white ceiling being put to.

But for the beautiful experiment of lying in bed I might never have discovered it. For years I have been looking for some blank spaces in a modern house to draw on. Paper is much too small for any really allegorical design; as Cyrano de Bergerac says: *"Il me faut des geants."* But when I tried to find these fine clear spaces in the modern rooms such as we all live in I was continually disappointed. I found an endless pattern and complication of small objects hung like a curtain of fine links between me and my desire. I examined the walls; I found them to my surprise to be already covered with wall-paper, and I found the wall-paper to be already covered with very uninteresting images, all bearing a ridiculous resemblance to each other. I could not understand why one arbitrary symbol (a symbol apparently entirely devoid of any religious or philosophical significance) should thus be sprinkled all over my nice walls like a sort of small-pox. The Bible must be referring to wall-papers, I think, when it says, "Use not vain repetitions, as the Gentiles do." I found the Turkey carpet a mass of unmeaning colors, rather like the Turkish Empire, or like the sweetmeat called Turkish Delight. I do not exactly know what Turkish Delight really is; but I suppose it is Macedonian

Massacres. Everywhere that I went with my pencil or my
paint brush, I found that others had unaccountably been
before me, spoiling the walls, the curtains, and the furniture with their childish and barbaric designs.

Nowhere did I find a really clear space for sketching until this occasion when I prolonged beyond the proper limit
the process of lying on my back in bed. Then the light of
that white heaven broke upon my vision, that breadth of
mere white which is indeed almost the definition of Paradise, since it means purity and also means freedom. But
alas! like all heavens, now that it is seen it is found to be un-
attainable: it looks more austere and more distant than the
blue sky outside the window. For my proposal to paint on it
with the bristly end of a broom has been discouraged —
never mind by whom; by a person debarred from all political rights — and even my minor proposal to put the other
end of the broom into the kitchen fire and turn it into
charcoal has not been conceded. Yet I am certain that it was
from persons in my position that all the original inspiration came from covering the ceilings of palaces and cathedrals with a riot of fallen angels or victorious gods. I am
sure that it was only because Michelangelo was engaged in
the ancient and honorable occupation of lying in bed that
he ever realized how the roof of the Sistine Chapel might
be made into an awful imitation of a divine drama that
could only be acted in the heavens.

The tone now commonly taken towards the practice of
lying in bed is hypocritical and unhealthy. Of all the marks
of modernity that seem to mean a kind of decadence, there
is none more menacing and dangerous than the exaltation
of very small and secondary matters of conduct at the expense of very great and primary ones, at the expense of

eternal ties and tragic human morality. If there is one thing worse than the modern weakening of major morals it is the modern strengthening of minor morals. Thus it is considered more withering to accuse a man of bad taste than of bad ethics. Cleanliness is not next to godliness nowadays, for cleanliness is made an essential and godliness is regarded as an offense. A playwright can attack the institution of marriage so long as he does not misrepresent the manners of society, and I have met Ibsenite pessimists who thought it wrong to take beer but right to take prussic acid. Especially this is so in matters of hygiene; notably such matters as lying in bed. Instead of being regarded, as it ought to be, as a matter of personal convenience and adjustment, it has come to be regarded by many as if it were a part of essential morals to get up early in the morning. It is, upon the whole, part of practical wisdom; but there is nothing good about it or bad about its opposite.

Misers get up early in the morning; and burglars, I am informed, get up the night before. It is the great peril of our society that all its mechanism may grow more fixed while its spirit grows more fickle. A man's minor actions and arrangements ought to be free, flexible, creative; the things that should be unchangeable are his principles, his ideals. But with us the reverse is true; our views change constantly; but our lunch does not change. Now, I should like men to have strong and rooted conceptions, but as for their lunch, let them have it sometimes in the garden, sometimes in bed, sometimes on the roof, sometimes in the top of a tree. Let them argue from the same first principles, but let them do it in a bed, or a boat, or a balloon.

the Epicurean

Decadence that defies accepted morality, pleasures that destroy the senses, habits that compromise the temple of the soul; these are pursuits that befit no upstanding citizen or responsible adult unless they happen to be a worshiper of a deranged and priapic god. Or an idler, bored by the bathos of consciousness.

The epicurean tendencies of idlers are rife. The rejection of work — to deny all the responsibilities and banalities enforced by an employer — is a denial of the disagreeable. And so we dedicate the following section to those moments in life when there are no principles, only pleasure.

Be You Drunken!

BAUDELAIRE, 1869

As this splendid "prose poem in verse" shows, being drunk was the only feasible escape route from the shackles of time for the terminally depressed young Baudelaire.

One must always be drunk. That's all there is to it; that's the only solution. In order not to feel the horrible burden of

Time breaking your shoulders and bowing your head to the

ground, you must be drunken without respite.

But; with what? With wine, poetry or virtue, as you will.

Be you drunken.

And if sometimes you awake, on the steps of a palace, in

the green herbage of a ditch or in the dreary solitude of your

room, then ask the wind, the waves, the stars, the birds, the

clocks, ask everything that runs, that moans, that moves

on wheels, everything that sings and speaks — ask them what

is the time of day; and the wind, the waves, the stars, the

birds and the clocks will answer you: It is time to get

drunk. In order not to be the martyred slave of Time, be you

drunken; be you drunken ceaselessly! With wine, poetry or

virtue, as you will!

from *Miles: The Autobiography*
WITH QUINCEY TROUPE, 1989

He may be the greatest jazz trumpeter of the century, but Miles Davis wasn't always working hard. In fact, as the following extract describes, sensual pleasures replaced music for a while.

*F*rom 1975 until early 1980 I didn't pick up my horn; for over four years, didn't pick it up once. I would walk by and look at it, then think about trying to play. But after a while I didn't even do that. It just went out of my mind because I was involved in doing other things; other things which mostly weren't good for me. But I did them anyway and, looking back, I don't have any guilt about doing them.

I had been involved in music continuously since I was twelve or thirteen years old. It was all I thought about, all I lived for, all I completely loved. I had been obsessed with it for thirty-six or thirty-seven straight years, and at forty-nine years of age, I needed a break from it, needed another perspective on everything I was doing in order to make a clean start and pull my life back together again. I wanted to play music, but I wanted to play it differently than I had in the past and I also wanted to play in big halls *all* the time instead of in little jazz clubs. For the time being, I was through with playing little jazz clubs because my music and its requirements had just outgrown them.

My health was also a factor, and it was getting harder and harder for me to play constantly like I was because my hip wasn't getting any better. I hated limping around the stage like I was, being in all that pain and taking all them drugs. It was a drag. I have a lot of pride in myself and in the way I look, the way I present myself. So I didn't like the way

I was physically, and didn't like people looking at me with all that pity in their eyes. I couldn't stand that shit, man.

I couldn't play two weeks in a club without having to go to the hospital. Drinking so much, snorting all the time, and fucking all night. You can't do all of that and create music like you want to. You got to do one or the other. Artie Shaw told me one time, "Miles, you can't play that third concert in bed." What he meant was that if you do two concerts and you're doing all that other stuff, then that third concert you're supposed to play when you're doing one-nighters is going to be played in bed because you're going to be wasted. After a while, all that fucking ain't nothing but tits and asses and pussy. After a while there is no emotion in it because I put so much emotion into my music. The only reason I didn't get staggering drunk was because when I played all that shit came out of my pores. I never did get drunk when I drank a lot, but I would throw up the next day at exactly twelve noon. Tony Williams would come by some time in the morning and at 11:55 he would say, "Okay, Miles, you got exactly five minutes before it's time for you to throw up." And then he'd leave the room and I would go into the bathroom at exactly twelve o'clock and throw up.

Then there was the business side of the music industry, which is very tough and demanding and racist. I didn't like the way I was being treated by Columbia and by people who owned the jazz clubs. They treat you like a slave because they're giving you a little money, especially if you're black. They treated all their white stars like they were kings or queens, and I just hated that shit, especially since they were stealing all their shit from black music and trying to act black. Record companies were still pushing their white shit over all the black music and they *knew* that they had taken it from black people. But they didn't care. All the record companies were interested in at that time was making a lot of money and keeping their so-called black stars on the music plantation so that their white stars could just rip us off. All that just made me sicker than I was physically, made me sick spiritually, and so I just dropped out.

I had invested my money pretty good and Columbia still paid me for a couple of years while I was out of the music industry. We worked out a deal so that they could keep me on the label, and that was cool enough to keep some money coming from royalties. In the seventies, my deal with Columbia was that I got over a million dollars to deliver albums, plus royalties. Plus I had a few rich white ladies who saw to it that I didn't want for money. Mostly during those four or five years that I was out of music, I just took a lot of cocaine (about $500 a day at one point) and fucked all the women I could get into my house. I was also addicted to pills, like Percodan and Seconal, and I was drinking a lot, Heinekens and cognac. Mostly I snorted coke, but sometimes I would inject coke and heroin into my leg: it's called a speedball and it was what killed John Belushi. I didn't go out too often and when I did it was mostly to after-hours places up in Harlem where I just kept on getting high and living from day to day.

I'm not the best person in the world about picking up after myself and keeping a house clean and neat because I didn't never have to do any of that stuff. When I was young, either my mother or my sister, Dorothy, did it, and later my father had a maid. I've always been clean about my personal hygiene, but the other shit I never learned to do and, frankly, I didn't even think about doing it. When I started living by myself after I broke up with Frances, Cicely, Betty, Marguerite, and Jackie, the maids who I had during this time just stopped coming, I guess because of how crazy I was acting. They were probably afraid to be alone with me. I would have a maid from time to time but I couldn't keep anyone steady because cleaning up after me got to be a very big job. The house was a wreck, clothes everywhere, dirty dishes in the sink, newspapers and magazines all over the floor, beer bottles and garbage and trash everywhere. The roaches had a field day. Sometimes I would get someone to come in or one of my girlfriends would do it, but mostly the house was filthy and real dark and gloomy, like a dungeon. I didn't give a fuck because I never thought about it, except during those very few times that I was sober.

I became a hermit, hardly ever going outside. My only connection with the outside world was mostly through watching television — which was on around the clock — and the newspapers and magazines I was reading. Sometimes I got information from a few old friends who would drop by to see me to see if everything was all right, like Max Roach, Jack DeJohnette, Jackie Battle, Al Foster, Gil Evans (I saw Gil and Al more than anybody else), Dizzy Gillespie, Herbie Hancock, Ron Carter, Tony Williams, Philly Joe Jones, Richard Pryor, and Cicely Tyson. I got a lot of information from them but sometimes I wouldn't even let them come in.

I changed managers again through this period. I hired Mark Rothbaum, who had worked for my former manager Neil Reshen for a while, and later became Willie Nelson's manager. My road manager, Jim Rose, was around.

But the person who was around the most after a while and who ran errands for me was a young black guy named Eric Engles, who I knew through his mother. Eric stayed with me most of the time during those silent years. If I didn't cook for myself or if one of my girlfriends didn't, Eric would run up to the Cellar, my friend Howard Johnson's place, and get me some fried chicken. It was good that I had Eric because there were times during this period when I didn't leave my house for six months or more.

When my old friends came by to see how I was living they would be shocked. But they didn't say nothing because I think they were afraid if they had, I would just put them out, which I would have. After a while many of my old musician friends stopped coming by, because a lot of time I wouldn't let them in. They got sick and tired of that shit so they just stopped coming. When all those rumors got out about me doing a lot of drugs during that time they were all on the money, because I was. Sex and drugs took the place that music had occupied in my life until then and I did both of them around the clock.

I had so many different women during this period that I lost track of most of them and don't even remember their names. If I met them on the street today I probably wouldn't even recognize most of them. They were there one night and gone the next day and that was that. Most of them are just a blur. Toward the end of my silent period, Cicely Tyson came back into my love life, although she had always been a friend and I would see her from time to time. Jackie Battle came by to check on me, but we were no longer lovers, just real good friends.

I was interested in what some people would call kinky sex, you know, getting it on in bed sometimes with more than one woman. Or sometimes I would watch them just freaking out on themselves. I enjoyed it, I ain't going to lie about that. It gave me a thrill — and during this period I was definitely into thrills.

———

from *Barthes on Barthes*
ROLAND BARTHES, 1975

The French philosopher wasn't above a bit of slobbing around every now and then. Luckily, he deconstructed that desire for us.

l'Aise — Ease

*B*eing a hedonist (since he regards himself as one), he seeks a state which is, really, comfort; but this comfort is more complicated than the household kind whose elements are determined by our society: it is a comfort he arranged for himself (the way my grandfather B., at the end of his life, had arranged a little platform inside his window, so as to obtain a better view of the garden while he was working). This personal comfort might be called: *ease*. Ease can be given a theoretical dignity ("We need not keep our distance with regard to formalism, merely our ease"), and also an ethical force: it is the deliberate loss of all heroism, *even in pleasure.*

———

from *Against Nature*
J.-K. HUYSMANS, 1884

A classic of decadent literature, Huysmans' hero Des Esseintes, driven by his conviction that travel was a waste of time, was an early experimenter in virtual reality of the most exquisite kind.

*O*n autumn evenings, when the samovar stood steaming on the table and the sun had almost set, the water in the aquarium which had been dull and turbid all morning, would turn red like glowing embers and shed a fiery, glimmering light upon the pale walls.

Sometimes of an afternoon, when Des Esseintes happened to be already up and about, he would set in action the system of pipes and conduits which emptied the aquarium and refilled it with fresh water, and then pour in a few drops of colored essences, thus producing at will the various tints, green or grey, opaline or silvery, which real rivers take on according to the color of the sky, the greater or less brilliance of the sun's rays, the more or less imminent threat of rain – in a word, according to the season and the weather.

He could then imagine himself between-decks in a brig, and gazed inquisitively at some ingenious mechanical fishes driven by clockwork, which moved backwards and forwards behind the port-hole window and got entangled in artificial seaweed. At other times, while he was inhaling the smell of tar which had been introduced into the room before he entered it, he would examine a series of color-prints on the walls, such as you see in packetboat offices and Lloyd's agencies, representing steamers bound for Valparaiso and the River Plate, alongside framed notices giving the itineraries of the Royal Mail Steam Packet Line and the Lopez and Valéry Companies, as well as the freight charges and ports of call of the transatlantic mail-boats.

Then, when he was tired of consulting these time-tables, he would rest his eyes by looking at the chronometers and compasses, the sextants and dividers, the binoculars and charts scattered about on a side-table which was dominated by a single book, bound in sea calf leather: the *Narrative of Arthur Gordon Pym*, specially printed for him on laid paper of pure linen, hand picked and bearing a seagull water-mark.

Finally he could take stock of the fishing-rods, the brown-tanned nets, the rolls of russet-colored sails and the miniature anchor made of cork painted black, all piled higgledy-piggledy beside the door that led to the kitchen by way of a corridor padded, like the passage between dining-room and study, in such a way as to absorb any noises and smells.

By these means he was able to enjoy quickly, almost simultaneously, all the sensations of a long sea-voyage, without ever leaving home; the pleasure of moving from place to place, a pleasure which in fact exists only in recollection of the past and hardly ever in experience of the present, this pleasure he could savor in full and in comfort, without fatigue or worry, in this cabin whose deliberate disorder, impermanent appearance, and makeshift appointments corresponded fairly closely to the flying visits he paid it and the limited time he gave his meals, while it offered a complete contrast to his study, a permanent, orderly, well-established room, admirably equipped to maintain and uphold a stay-at-home existence.

Travel, indeed, struck him as being a waste of time, since he believed that the imagination could provide a more-than-adequate substitute for the vulgar reality of actual experience. In his opinion it was perfectly possible to fulfill those desires commonly supposed to be the most difficult to satisfy under normal conditions, and this by the trifling subterfuge of producing a fair imitation of the object of those desires. Thus it is well known that nowadays, in res-

taurants famed for the excellence of their cellars, the gour-
mets go into raptures over rare vintages manufactured out
of cheap wines treated according to Monsieur Pasteur's
method. Now, whether they are genuine or faked, these
wines have the same aroma, the same color, the same bou-
quet; and consequently the pleasure experienced in tasting
these factitious, sophisticated beverages is absolutely identical with that which would be afforded by the pure, un-
adulterated wine, now unobtainable at any price.

There can be no doubt that by transferring this ingenious trickery, this clever simulation to the intellectual
plane, one can enjoy, just as easily as on the material plane,
imaginary pleasures similar in all respects to the pleasures
of reality; no doubt, for instance, that anyone can go on
long voyages of exploration sitting by the fire, helping out
his sluggish or refractory mind, if the need arises, by dip-
ping into some book describing travels in distant lands; no
doubt, either, that without stirring out of Paris it is possible
to obtain the health-giving impression of sea-bathing – for
all that this involves is a visit to the Bain Vigier, an estab-
lishment to be found on a pontoon moored in the middle
of the Seine.

There, by salting your bath-water and adding sulfate of
soda with hydrochlorate of magnesium and lime in the
proportions recommended by the Pharmacopoeia; by
opening a box with a tight-fitting screw-top and taking out
a ball of twine or a twist of rope, bought for the occasion
from one of those enormous roperies whose warehouses
and cellars reek with the smell of the sea and sea-ports; by
breathing in the odors which the twine or the twist of rope
is sure to have retained; by consulting a life-like photo-
graph of the casino and zealously reading the *Guide Joanne*

describing the beauties of the seaside resort where you would like to be; by letting yourself be lulled by the waves created in your bath by the backwash of the paddle-steamers passing close to the pontoon; by listening to the moaning of the wind as it blows under the arches of the Pont Royal and the dull rumble of the buses crossing the bridge just a few feet over your head; by employing these simple devices, you can produce an illusion of seabathing which will be undeniable, convincing, and complete.

The main thing is to know how to set about it, to be able to concentrate your attention on a single detail, to forget yourself sufficiently to bring about the desired hallucination and so substitute the vision of a reality for the reality itself.

As a matter of fact, artifice was considered by Des Esseintes to be the distinctive mark of human genius.

Nature, he used to say, has had her day; she has finally and utterly exhausted the patience of sensitive observers by the revolting uniformity of her landscapes and skyscapes. After all, what platitudinous limitations she imposes, like a tradesman specializing in a single line of business; what petty-minded restrictions, like a shopkeeper stocking one article to the exclusion of all others; what a monotonous store of meadows and trees, what a commonplace display of mountains and seas!

In fact, there is not a single one of her inventions, deemed so subtle and sublime, that human ingenuity cannot manufacture; no moonlit Forest of Fontainebleau that cannot be reproduced by stage scenery under floodlighting; no cascade that cannot be imitated to perfection by hydraulic engineering; no rock that papier-mâché cannot counterfeit; no flower that carefully chosen taffeta and delicately colored paper cannot match!

There can be no shadow of doubt that with her never-ending platitudes the old crone has by now exhausted the good-humored admiration of all true artists, and the time has surely come for artifice to take her place whenever possible.

Eight Miles High

WILL SELF, 1995

If you really must travel by air, then at least get yourself upgraded to first class. As Will Self discovered, this is a pleasure without peer.

Make no mistake about it, first class flying is the heroin of travel. A few flights might not give you a bad yen, but push it too far and you'll never, ever escape the consequences: your metabolism will alter at a cellular level; you'll have to become rich — or a whore. Fuck it, I've only had one hit of this shit and I'm still swaddled in its velvet paw ten days later.

But — ah, how did you start? I mean, did someone give it to you, or what?

It's like this: I've been up all night at the fag end of a rolled-up 72 hours of missed obligations, street corner burns and tiffs with desk clerks. My face is a kind of *impasto* of willed disintegration, and I'm checking in for the Saturday p.m. Virgin flight to New York. I've spent the last twenty hours spreading myself around town like some kind of new, err . . . spread. Pulling the carriage of my body into bar-after-bar-after-bar on those most exiguous of rails, the ones just thick enough to get you to . . . the bar. I'm feeling my gusset — it's feeling me. I'm also sensing the airport as a gusset — soiled of course. See those baggage conveyors, how they yaw and grab at the air's damp perineum . . . I'm all fucked up. It's not funny.

There's a gusset in front of me for the mid-class check in. Except I don't think it's called mid-class any more, it's called something like priority class. They've euphemized the shit out of it. How like Major's Britain. Perhaps Virgin Atlantic is a microcosm of Major's Britain. The gusset in front of me is wearing brown Terylene trousers and the body of a largish Asian man. Ahead of him some old gusset is buying a ticket. It's taking several millennia, Ancient Sumer has risen once more, Gilgamesh appears on the cover of *Radio Times*. Inside my trousers a rain forest is being established, an entire ecosystem. Miniature Colobus monkeys swing from the hairs on my testicles.

I start to study the staff behind the desk. They are wearing beautifully neat uniforms in bright, bright primary colors. They are young and shapely. Their faces are not willed *impastos* of disintegration. The last rail they rode on was Network South East. Their pants are uniformly gussetless. They look like heavenly extras in a remake of *A Matter of Life and Death*. I approach the white-clad senior angel and cough up some sort of gurgle of discontent. She beckons me round to the Upper Class check in. And then it starts, the plunger is pressed home: the slippery descent into bliss.

The desk clerk slaps and tickles the keyboard, his lovely brow furrows, he can't hack it. He looks up and says: "I'm sorry Mr. Self, we have no mid-class seats left, we'll have to bump you up to Upper Class . . . " He's *sorry!* I do nothing but splutter, and stand there while he goes on slapping and caressing the molded plastic for about twenty seconds real time (the Queen Mother goes on mega-H.R.T. and is artificially inseminated, the donor is Phil Collins, the intention: to beget a master race . . .). It's too much for me to bear; deranged at the prospect I attempt to run off in the direction of the aircraft, until called back to get a boarding card.

He's thanking me. I'm thanking him. This is a little darling slice of luck. I don't know what's in store yet, but even now I'd give the most fulsome encomiums to VA. Best Airline 1995? Fuck it: Best Airline of the Whole Fucking Decade. And if I knew then what I know now? No encomium would suffice. If necessary I'd go round to Richard Branson's house, or barge, or whatever it is, and rim him to get another seat in Upper Class.

Then I'm clunking through something called "fast track." Not, as I had hoped, a kind of super-rail, running incandescently ahead of my stooped membranes, but really a taped-off extra lane along which the rich limp, burdened by their responsibilities. It has its own metal detectors and security and apparently its own immigration officials. Truly, wealth is another country.

Then, ahead of me stretch more wavering, vibrating gussets. Giant, black gussets along which passenger-guests yomp. My gate is so far away that I may have to take on bearers. I'm flagging, when another Virgin seraphim appears driving one of those little rubber-wheeled trolleys. "Virgin Atlantic sir?" I assent. "Hop on." And we're off. I've prematurely aged to this extent: being carted around Heathrow like some thyroid case on a fork-lift. The faces of

the healthy, as we pass them, register amusement and contempt. But I don't care, I've lanced into an Arcadia of the
idle. We approach the gate, the seraphim says, "have your
boarding card ready please," and then we almost drive *on to*
the plane. I totter off the trolley, the cherubim at the door
examines my boarding card and directs me all of eight feet
to my seat.

I say seat, but really this is a terrible misnomer. It isn't a
seat — it's a *bed*. Another heavenly chore-whore appears
and sort of tucks me into this thing. "Champagne, orange
juice, or buck's fizz?" she asks. I opt — unsurprisingly — for
champagne, and she brings me an *entire bottle* of Tattinger
brut. This I cradle protectively, a child safe with its teddy
bear in its cot, as we lumber along the runway and take off.

Take-off is always a big disappointment for me. Of
course, there is always the sensation of being wrenched
from the earth as if the plane were God's friction toy, and
He a child determined to break it. This is never entirely vi-
tiated by the fact that modern 747s are bigger than
Chartres, with whole transepts and choirs full of gussets
playing *Donkey Kong* and reading novels by Jeffrey Archer.
We still know the sublime is somewhere out there.

During take-off I often console myself with imagining
how John Marten, the great 19th century apocalyptic
painter (check out his *Plains of Heaven* and *The Fall of Babylon* in
the Tate) would deal with the depiction of the interior of a
Virgin 747, as its nose rammed into some reservoir in
Staines at 32 feet per second/per second. The buckling of
entire phalanxes of mortgage brokers and PE teachers
could only really be satisfactorily achieved using oils.
Thick, thick oils.

I'm mature enough to understand that air travel has to be rendered thus: from check-in, through terminal, to aircraft itself, a kind of illimitable boredom of corporate design. The point being that flying – even in 747s – is intrinsically *so* exciting, that everything must be done to make it dull. That's why there aren't full-length windows, or transparent floors. That's why the steward(esse)s don't wear Buck Rogers-style uniforms and shout "Wheeeee!" during take-off. That's why the pilot doesn't come on the PA as you're taxiing and say something like the following:

"Hi! I'm Dave, your pilot this afternoon for our flight to New York. We're taxiing down to Runway Four, and personally I'm as wired-up as a baboon on methedrine. Shit, I'm going to hit that throttle and we're going to have over two million pounds of thrust jamming up our arses before you can say 'Richard Gere.' If you really want to wrap your head around the event-horizon of take-off, keep your eyes on the video screens, we're going to be relaying a set of deeply strange trance-enhancement graphics that will make the *Beyond the Parhelion* section of *2001* look like a broken lava lamp. Clamp on those earphones and clock the Mad Professor's remix of *Interstellar Overdrive*; and when those oxygen masks fall into your lap be sure to take a good long blast – it's specially formulated Virgin DMT. I think you'll agree with me: it's the food of the gods. Remember, every flight with Virgin is a profound, collective drug ritual. Here weee goooooo!"

No. None of the above.

Then we're airborne. We level off (I say that advisedly – I've been leveled off for some years), and the "no smoking" sign winks out. I spark up. I'm at 22,000 feet, and I'm smoking and drinking in *bed*. A senior sort of *putti* appears. In a

New York accent, she asks me if I would like a cocktail. Asks me by name. Asks me as if my welfare really concerns her.

And not just my current welfare, I feel she knows my whole poignant history intimately, just from the tone of her voice. I feel she was with me in the playground when that 13-year-old thug took the piss out of my zip-up, suede ankle-boots; and then when I called him out on it, beat me to a reasonable pulp. I whimper, choking back the appellation "Mummy," that I would like a Bloody Mary. "Is that with Tabasco and celery salt Mr. Self, or would you prefer a more Worcester sauce-oriented version?" I like it here.

I'm going to crash soon. I can do that here. I've got a window "seat," but there's enough space between my bed and the aisle bed that I can walk around the end of it without even getting near to the feet of its occupant. Damn it, the guy in the next-door bed is so far away that I could have one of my full-scale *Jacob's Ladder*-type nightmares, complete with arm-thrashing and convulsions, without him even noticing.

There's that, and there's the blissful absence of the video screens as well. They've been stowed somewhere in the interstices of the beds for take-off, and need never be pulled out again. That's fine by me. I've never been able to cope with those miniature LCD video screens since the time I got on a Virgin flight to New York — admittedly well over the herbaceous border — and became convinced that they were accurately portraying the thoughts of the person sitting in the seat in front of me.

Needless to say, it didn't surprise me in the least to learn that at the core of the very being of the woman sitting in front of me, Mick Jagger pranced, wearing a leather jacket that had last seen service in an episode of *BMX Bandits*.

When I awake, we're beginning our descent. Mummy appears next to my bed and says: "Diddums haveums a nice sleepums?" Touchdown is as slight as a repressed homosexual vice cop putting the cuffs on a rent boy. I swing my feet out of bed and stroll off the aircraft, waving goodbye to my close, close Virgin friends. I'm through immigration and customs with indecent haste. Why? Because I'm the first fucker off the entire plane.

I'm in a cab, jolting along the Van Eyck Expressway, watching lissom black kids shoot hoops outside frame houses before you can say Martin Scorsese. It's all been such a painless progress that I cannot believe I'm actually in New York, until the cabbie (who's a Haitian or some such), on discovering that I write fiction for a living, inquires with great seriousness: "Say, this thing called 'Writer's Block'. Does it really exist or what?"

<hr />

from *A Season in Hell*

ARTHUR RIMBAUD, 1874

Rimbaud was only twenty when he wrote of his wimpish but lecherous character, and hatred of work. Good lad, we say.

I inherit from my Gaulish ancestors my whitish-blue eye, my narrow skull, and my lack of skill in fighting. My attire seems to me as barbarous as theirs. But I don't butter my hair.

The Gauls were the clumsiest flayers of cattle and burners of grass of their epoch.

From them I have: idolatry and love of sacrilege — oh! every vice, anger, lechery — magnificent, lechery — above all, mendacity and sloth.

I loathe all trades. Masters and servants — all — peasants, base. The hand with the pen is no better than the hand on the plough — What an age of hands! — I shall never get my hand in. And then servitude leads too far. The honesty of beggary breaks my heart. Criminals disgust me like eunuchs: as for me, I am entire, and I don't care.

But! who made my tongue so perfidious that it has been able until now to guide and protect my laziness? Without using even my body to make a living, and idler than a toad, I have lived everywhere. Not a family in Europe that I don't know — I mean families like mine, who owe everything to the declaration of the Rights of Man — I've known every young man of good family! If only I had antecedents at some point or other in the history of France!

But no; nothing.

It is perfectly evident to me that I have always belonged to an inferior race. I don't understand rebellion. My race never rebelled except to loot: as hyenas devour an animal they have not killed.

I remember the history of France, eldest daughter of the Church. I would have made, as a villein, the journey to the Holy Land; I have in my head all the roads in the Swabian plains, as well as views of Byzantium, and of the ramparts of Suleiman. The cult of the Virgin Mary, and compassion for the crucified one, awaken in me among a thousand profane enchantments — I sit, stricken with leprosy, on potsherds and nettles at the foot of a wall ravaged by the sun — Later, as a mercenary, I should have bivouacked under the night skies of Germany.

Ah! again: I am dancing the witches' sabbath in a red glade, with old women and children.

I do not remember anything more distant than this country and Christianity. I should never have enough of seeing myself in this past. But always alone; without family; what language, even, did I speak? I never see myself in Christ's counsels; nor in the counsels of the Lords — Christ's representatives.

What was I in the last century? I only find myself today. No more wanderers, no more vague wars. The inferior race has spread everywhere — the people, as they say; reason, nationality, science.

Oh! science! Everything has been revised. For the body and for the soul — the viaticum — we have medicine and philosophy — old wives' remedies and arrangements of popular songs. As well as the amusements of princes and the games which they forbade! Geography, cosmography, mechanics, chemistry! . . .

Science, the new aristocracy! Progress. The world is on the march! Why shouldn't it turn, too?

It is the vision of numbers. We are moving toward the *Spirit*. It is absolutely certain, it is the voice of the oracle, what I say. I understand, and, not knowing how to express myself without pagan words, I would prefer to remain silent.

Pagan blood returns! The Spirit is near. Why does Christ not help me by giving my soul nobility and freedom? Alas! the Gospel has passed by! the Gospel! the Gospel.

I await God greedily. I have been of inferior race from all eternity.

Here I am on the Breton shore. How the towns light up in the evening. My day is done; I am leaving Europe. The sea air will scorch my lungs; lost climates will tan my skin.

I shall swim, stamp down the grass, hunt, above all smoke;
I shall drink liquors as strong as boiling metal — as my dear
ancestors did, round their fires.

I shall return with limbs of iron, dark skin, a furious eye:
from my mask, I shall be judged as belonging to a mighty
race. I shall have gold: I shall be idle and brutal. Women
take care of these ferocious invalids returned from hot
countries. I shall be involved in politics. Saved.

At present I am damned, I loathe the fatherland. The
best thing of all is a good drunken sleep on the beach.

---

from *The Ruba'iyat of Omar Khayyam (d. 1122)*

Antipathy to work and a love of wine, women and song is nothing new, as we discover in this extract from the classic Persian poem.

64

Drink wine since for our destruction
The firmament has got its eye on our precious souls;
Sit where it is green and enjoy the sparkling liquor,
Because this grass will grow nicely from your dust and
    mine.

65

I saw a man working on a building site,
He was stamping down the clay;
The clay protested,
"Stop it, you like me will be stamped on by many a
    foot."

66

Oh heart-seeker raise the cup and the jug,
Go back to the meadows on the stream's verge:
This wheel has made many a radiant-cheeked, idol-
     form
Over and over again into cups and jugs.

67

Last night I smashed an earthenware pot on the stones,
I was drunk when I committed this folly:
The pot protested,
"I was like you, you will be like me also."

68

From that wine-jug which has no harm in it,
Fill a bowl, boy, drink and pass it to me,
Before, by some wayside,
A potter uses your clay and mine for just such a jug.

69

I passed by a potter the day before last,
He was ceaselessly plying his skill with the clay,
And, what the blind do not see, I could —
My father's clay in every potter's hand.

70

Stop potter, if you have any sense,
How long will you debase man's clay?
You have put Feridun's finger and Kaikhosrau's hand
On the wheel — what do you think you're doing?

71

I watched a potter in his work-place,
Saw the master, his foot on the wheel's treddle;
Unabashed, he was making a jug's lid and handle
From a king's head and a beggar's hand.

72

This jug was love-sick like me,
Tangled in a fair girl's locks;
This handle you now see on its neck
Was his hand on the neck of the girl.

73

I was in the potter's shop last night,
And saw two thousand jugs, some speaking, some
    dumb;
Each was anxiously asking,
"Where is the potter, and the buyer and seller of pots?"

74

If I'm drunk on forbidden wine, so I am!
And if I'm an unbeliever, a pagan or idolater, so I am!
Every sect has its own suspicions of me,
I myself am just what I am.

75

My rule of life is to drink and be merry,
To be free from belief and unbelief is my religion:
I asked the Bride of Destiny her bride-price,
"Your joyous heart," she said.

76

I cannot live without the sparkling vintage,
Cannot bear the body's burden without wine:
I am a slave to that last gasp when the wine-server says,
"Have another," and I can't.

77

Tonight I will make a tun of wine,
Set myself up with two bowls of it;
First I will divorce absolutely reason and religion;
Then take to wife the daughter of the vine.

78

When I am dead, scatter my dust
And make my condition an example to men:
Moisten my dust with wine,
To make the seal on a vat out of my corpse.

79

Wash me in wine when I go,
For my burial service use a text concerning wine;
Would you find me on the Day of Doom,
Look for me in the dust at the wine-shop's door.

80

I drink so much wine, its aroma
Will rise from the dust when I'm under it;
Should a toper come upon my dust,
The fragrance from my corpse will make him roaring
    drunk.

81

The day when my life's branch is uprooted
And my members are dispersed,
Should my clay be used to make a cup
It would come to life as soon as it was filled with wine.

82

When I am prostrate at the feet of doom,
My hope of life torn up by the root,
Take care to use my clay only for a goblet –
The smell of wine might restore me life for a moment.

83

When you are in convivial company,
You must remember ardently your friend:
When you are drinking mellow wine together
And my turn comes, invert the glass.

84

The captives of intellect and of the nice distinction,
Worrying about Being and Non-Being themselves
    become nothing;
You with the news, go and seek out the juice of the
    vine,
Those without it wither before they're ripe.

85

Oh Canon Jurist, we work better than you,
With all this drunkenness, we're more sober:
You drink men's blood, we, the vine's,
Be honest – which of us is the more bloodthirsty?

86

A religious man said to a whore, "You're drunk,
Caught every moment in a different snare."
She replied, "Oh Shaikh, I am what you say,
Are you what you seem?"

87

They say lovers and drunkards go to hell,
A controversial dictum not easy to accept:
If the lover and drunkard are for hell,
Tomorrow Paradise will be empty.

88

They promise there will be Paradise and the houri-
    eyed,
Where clear wine and honey will flow:
Should we prefer wine and a lover, what's the harm?
Are not these the final recompense?

89

They say there is Paradise with the houris and the
    River,
Wine freshets, milk, sweets and honey:
Fill the wine-cup, put it in my hand —
Cash is better than a thousand promises.

90

They say houris make the gardens of Paradise delicious,
I say that the juice of the vine is delicious,
Take this cash and reject that credit —
The sound of a distant drum, brother, is sweet.

91

Nobody, heart, has seen heaven or hell,
Tell me, dear, who has returned from there?
Our hopes and fears are on something of which,
My dear, there is no indication but the name.

92

I do not know whether he who shaped me
Made me for heaven or grim hell:
A cup, a lover and music on the field's verge –
These three are my cash, heaven your I.O.U.

93

Since in this sphere we have no abiding place,
To be without wine and a lover is a mistake:
How long shall hopes and fears persist whether the
     world
is created or eternal?
When I am gone, created and eternal worlds are the
     same.

94

Since at first my coming was not at my will,
And the going is involuntarily imposed,
Arise, fasten your belt brisk wine-boy,
I'll drown the world's sorrow in wine.

95

When life comes to an end it will be the same in
     Baghdad or Balkh,
When the cup brims over, it is the same if sweet or
     bitter:

Be glad, because after our time many a moon
Will grow full, and then wane.

96

Go only the way of tavern-roisterers,
Seek for girls, wine and music:
Wine-cup in hand, the wine-skin on the shoulder,
Drink the wine, my darling, and stop chattering . . .

104

I saw a waster sitting on a patch of ground,
Heedless of belief and unbelief, the world and the faith —
No God, no Truth, no Divine Law, no Certitude:
Who in either of the worlds has the courage of this
     man?

———◆———

Labor of Love

SUZANNE MOORE, 1995

Guardian columnist Suzanne Moore rhapsodizes about the pleasures of sex with no effort — just let the other person do the work.

You don't need me to tell you, I'm sure, that you don't learn how to have sex from doing it with boys, but from talking about it with girls. One girl in particular played a vital part in my sex education. Her name was Janice and she was the acknowledged expert in the field, primarily because she had found a copy of *How to be a Sensuous Woman* under her Dad's bed and therefore possessed the key to all knowledge. Another and somewhat unlikely pinnacle of aspiration was provided by that other key text of the time — *Deep Throat*. Although in theory we hoped, by chance, to locate a spare clitoris in our gullet, in practice none of us had ever given a blow job – apart from Janice, who not only knew how to do this but also claimed that she could perform something called "The Butterfly Flick." This was but one of the revolting things Janice could do. Another was to pile pure white "highlighter" into the arch of her artificial eyebrows. She had, in her quest to be a sensuous woman, shaved off her eyebrows and redrawn them halfway up her forehead. Advanced, I believe, is the word. There just wasn't the space between my eyelid and eyebrow in which to apply the requisite amount of gunk. Serious sensuality was beyond my reach.

I suppose that is why she took me in hand. Up in the bedroom of her parents' council house she turned the lights off, put on a red dress and a Barry White record and told me to shut up. She said if only you tried hard enough it was possible to come just listening to Barry. We spent many a night lying two foot apart on twin beds, fists clenched, eyes shut tight while Janice began to writhe and I replayed my then most trustworthy sexual fantasy – that I was an alien life form beamed aboard the Starship Enterprise, having to be examined by Kirk, Spock, and on a good night various others of the crew. Barry moaned in the background, Janice groaned in the foreground and I tried to steer my thoughts away from Bones and McCoy. There was still nothing doing and so it was that the first orgasm I ever faked was for a girl and not a boy. So much more demanding.

When I saw her years later she had taken up karate and was a hostess in a Japanese nightclub. She came to meet me wearing a glittery boob tube and evening gloves to show off her new pumped up biceps. "Don't I look amazing," she announced. I nodded. "I look like fucking Wonder Woman." That night she was sent home from the club to get changed because her appearance had frightened the Japanese businessmen. Oh Janice, where are you now? The point is that I know exactly where you are. You are a P.E. teacher living in Mile End. And that I guess is the moral of this story. What Janice tried to impress on me was that sex was an activity that you had to work at, practice, evolve techniques for: one vast exercise in self-improvement. I had never liked sports of any description. I was lazy. I couldn't be bothered.

But it wasn't just Janice that was filling my head full of this rubbish. It was everywhere I turned. *Cosmopolitan* and all the other women's magazines were, and still are, full of endless lists of what makes people good in bed, lists of activities that we should explore, experiment with. Recipes for love. Food that we can rub over each other, bits and bobs that can spice up our sex lives, advice on foreplay, afterplay, any old play at all as long as you are in touch with your fantasies, his fantasies, her fantasies, your next door neighbor's dog's fantasies.

Go into a porn shop and these fantasies are categorized with increasing fastidiousness. The sexual imagination is not limitless, just a repertoire of clichés. Are you the pisser or the pissed on? May I suggest something to go with your nipple clamps, madam? Some nipples perhaps. People moan about the sex industry but the point is that the commercial sex industry is tangential to most of our lives: we are all workers in a much bigger sex industry. Foucault may never have worn a "Queer as Fuck" T-shirt, but this much he understood: doing it, having it, getting it, wanting it is our duty, our task, our vocation. Boast of your idleness in other areas of your life, but not in this one. You may refuse to strive and drive but can you put your hand on your heart and say you are a sexual slacker? That you make the minimum effort both in and out of bed?

As we blame "the Sixties" and feminism for everything that has gone wrong in society, I will too. Once women were expected not to do too much. To lie back and think of England. Passivity was all that was expected and then, and as Mrs. Merton says, men waited a long time to hear those three magic words: "If you must."

Suddenly we started talking about female desire and women were obliged to swap passivity for activity. This was liberation. When pleasure is compulsory, an awful amount of effort is required. Some people noticed at the time that a lot of this female activity was in fact for the benefit of men. When we were uptight and repressed we could refuse sex or refuse to do much about it; once we were free to get in touch with our inner selves, guess what — our inner selves had always wanted to dress as French maids!

From that great leap forward we went on to endless discussions not of sex but of sexuality. You could have sex with texts. What a relief. I remember a particularly long tube ride with a well-known academic who got me up against the door while he expanded his theory of "vaginal openings." The textual juices flowed all right but our *jouissance* was rudely interrupted by our arrival at Cockfosters.

Still, at least such discussions were entirely meaningless. You were not expected to have a good time having them. Nowadays, the production and consumption of sexual energy has become a vast time and motion study. We are now obliged to have sex for the efficient functioning of our personalities. It is part of being a well-rounded person. Sex is as soothing as Nurofen and uses up calories too. It has become a kind of emotional All Bran. No wonder that the people who are most interesting to us sexually claim to be all bunged up like Morrissey. Madonna is of course living proof that you can try too hard. She has made sex as sexy as aerobics and, like step classes, something that has to be slotted into an already tight schedule.

Does Madonna spend days in bed with someone getting down to the real business – eating, sleeping, watching crap TV? Or does the sexiest woman in the world say "Sorry love, I've got to be at the gym in half an hour"? Idlers know the score here. They embrace all chemical impediments to sexual performance with almost tantric dedication. They understand the seduction of passivity and often find themselves not only too fucked up to fuck, but too fucked to give a fuck. This state of grace visits only the chosen few who truly know what it means to be bad in bed.

To be frank, I have never understood what was so wrong with lying back and thinking of England, apart, obviously, from worrying about contributing to the rise of nationalism. And I'm not the only one. When I expounded this theory to my omnisexual friend, Paul, he said: "Darling, that's all anyone ever wants – to lie there with a bottle of poppers jammed up one nostril while someone else does it to you." So why are we all so busy pretending that it's otherwise? Why are we still so bothered? When sex becomes such major toil, a labor of love, let me tell you it is your revolutionary duty to phone in sick.

———•◦•———

from *Don Juan*

LORD BYRON, 1819-24

Taken from Byron's rambling masterpiece, these cantos reveal a time when men spread themselves upon sofas of despair and sought those rare, peaceful corners from which all of life can be observed.

His morns he passed in business, which dissected,
Was like all business, a laborious nothing
That leads to lassitude, the most infected
And Centaur-Nessus garb of mortal clothing,
And on our sofas makes us lie dejected
And talk in tender horrors of our loathing
All kinds of toil, save for our country's good,
Which grows no better, though 'tis time it should.

His afternoons he passed in visits, luncheons,
Lounging, and boxing; and the twilight hour
In riding round those vegetable puncheons
Called parks, where there is neither fruit nor flower
Enough to gratify a bee's slight munchings.
But after all it is the only "bower"
(In Moore's phrase) where the fashionable fair
Can form a slight acquaintance with fresh air.

. . . Thrice happy he who, after a survey
Of the good company, can win a corner,
A door that's in or boudoir out of the way,
Where he may fix himself like small Jack Horner
And let the Babel round run as it may,
And look on as a mourner, or a scorner
Or an approver, or a mere spectator,
Yawning a little as the night grows later.

———◆———

from *Dr. Faustus*
CHRISTOPHER MARLOWE, 1593-1604

In our extract, Dr. Faustus is greeted by none other than Sloth, the sixth deadly sin, and for our money the most attractive.

FAUSTUS: ... What are thou, the sixth?
SLOTH: I am Sloth; I was begotten on a sunny bank, where I have lain ever since — and you have done me great injury to bring me from thence. Let me be carried thither again by Gluttony and Lechery. I'll not speak another word for a king's ransom.

———◆———

from *The Critic as Artist*
OSCAR WILDE, 1885

Ostensibly an essay advocating distance from mass life as a prerequisite of a critical mind, this extract makes a strong claim for the need of a contemplative population.

GILBERT: All art is immoral.
ERNEST: All art?
GILBERT: Yes. For emotion for the sake of emotion is the aim of art, and emotion for the sake of action is the aim of life, and of that practical organization of life that we call society. Society, which is the beginning and basis of morals, exists simply for the concentration of human energy, and in order to ensure its own continuance and healthy stability it demands, and no doubt rightly demands, of each of its citizens that he should contribute some form of produc-

tive labor to the common weal, and toil and travail that the day's work may be done. Society often forgives the criminal; it never forgives the dreamer. The beautiful sterile emotions that art excites in us are hateful in its eyes, and so completely are people dominated by the tyranny of this dreadful social ideal that they are always coming shamelessly up to one at Private Views and other places that are open to the general public, and saying in a loud stentorian voice, "What are you doing?" whereas "What are you thinking?" is the only question that any single civilized being should ever be allowed to whisper to another. They mean well, no doubt, these honest beaming folk. Perhaps that is the reason why they are so excessively tedious. But some one should teach them that while, in the opinion of society, Contemplation is the gravest sin of which any citizen can be guilty, in the opinion of the highest culture it is the proper occupation of man.

ERNEST: Contemplation?

GILBERT: Contemplation. I said to you some time ago that it was far more difficult to talk about a thing than to do it. Let me say to you now that to do nothing at all is the most difficult thing in the world, the most difficult and the most intellectual. To Plato, with his passion for wisdom, this was the noblest form of energy. To Aristotle, with his passion for knowledge, this was the noblest form of energy also. It was to this that the passion for holiness led the saint and the mystic of mediæval days.

ERNEST: We exist, then, to do nothing?

GILBERT: It is to do nothing that the elect exist. Action is limited and relative. Unlimited and absolute is the vision of him who sits at ease and watches, who walks in loneliness and dreams. But we who are born at the close of this won-

derful age are at once too cultured and too critical, too in-
tellectually subtle and too curious of exquisite pleasures,
to accept any speculations about life in exchange for life
itself. To us the *città divina* is colorless, and the *fruitio Dei*
without meaning. Metaphysics do not satisfy our temperaments, and religious ecstasy is out of date; The world
through which the Academic philosopher becomes "the
spectator of all time and of all existence" is not really an
ideal world, but simply a world of abstract ideas. When we
enter it, we starve amidst the chill mathematics of
thought. The courts of the city of God are not open to us
now. Its gates are guarded by Ignorance, and to pass them
we have to surrender all that in our nature is most divine.
It is enough that our fathers believed. They have exhausted
the faith-faculty of the species. Their legacy to us is the
skepticism of which they were afraid. Had they put it into
words, it might not live within us as thought. No, Ernest,
no. We cannot go back to the saint. There is far more to be
learned from the sinner. We cannot go back to the philosopher, and the mystic leads us astray. Who, as Mr. Pater sug-
gests somewhere, would exchange the curve of a single
rose-leaf for that formless intangible Being which Plato
rates so high? What to us is the Illumination of Philo, the
Abyss of Eckhart, the vision of Böhme, the monstrous
Heaven itself that was revealed to Swedenborg's blinded
eyes? Such things are less than the yellow trumpet of one
daffodil of the field, far less than the meanest of the visible
arts; for just as Nature is matter struggling into mind, so
Art is mind expressing itself under the conditions of matter, and thus, even in the lowliest of her manifestations,
she speaks to both sense and soul alike. To the æsthetic
temperament the vague is always repellent. The Greeks

were a nation of artists, because they were spared the sense of the infinite. Like Aristotle, like Goethe after he had read Kant, we desire the concrete, and nothing but the concrete can satisfy us.

ERNEST: What then do you propose?

GILBERT: It seems to me that with the development of the critical spirit we shall be able to realize, not merely our own lives, but the collective life of the race, and so to make ourselves absolutely modern, in the true meaning of the word modernity. For he to whom the present is the only thing that is present, knows nothing of the age in which he lives. To realize the nineteenth century, one must realize every century that has preceded it and that has contributed to its making. To know anything about oneself one must know all about others. There must be no mood with which one cannot sympathize, no dead mode of life that one cannot make alive. Is this impossible? I think not. By revealing to us the absolute mechanism of all action, and so freeing us from the self-imposed and trammelling burden of moral responsibility, the scientific principle of Heredity has become, as it were, the warrant for the contemplative life. It has shown us that we are never less free than when we try to act. It has hemmed us round with the nets of the hunter, and written upon the wall the prophecy of our doom. We may not watch it, for it is within us. We may not see it, save in a mirror that mirrors the soul. It is Nemesis without her mask. It is the last of the Fates, and the most terrible. It is the only one of the Gods whose real name we know.

And yet, while in the sphere of practical and external life it has robbed energy of its freedom and activity of its choice, in the subjective sphere, where the soul is at work, it comes to us, this terrible shadow, with many gifts in its hands, gifts of strange temperaments and subtle suscepti- bilities, gifts of wild ardors and chill moods of indifference, complex multiform gifts of thought that are at variance with each other, and passions that war against themselves. And so it is not our own life that we live, but the lives of the dead, and the soul that dwells within us is no single spiri- tual entity, making us personal and individual, created for our service, and entering into us for our joy. It is some- thing that has dwelt in fearful places, and in ancient sepul- chers has made its abode. It is sick with many maladies, and has memories of curious sins. It is wiser than we are, and its wisdom is bitter. It fills us with impossible desires, and makes us follow what we know we cannot gain. One thing, however, Ernest, it can do for us. It can lead us away from surroundings whose beauty is dimmed to us by the mist of familiarity, or whose ignoble ugliness and sordid claims are marring the perfection of our development. It can help us to leave the age in which we were born, and to pass into other ages, and find ourselves not exiled from their air. It can teach us how to escape from our experience, and to re- alize the experiences of those who are greater than we are. The pain of Leopardi crying out against life becomes our pain. Theocritus blows on his pipe, and we laugh with the lips of nymph and shepherd. In the wolfskin of Pierre Vidal we flee before the hounds, and in the armor of Lancelot we ride from the bower of the Queen. We have whispered the secret of our love beneath the cowl of Abelard, and in the stained raiment of Villon have put our shame into song. We can see the dawn through Shelley's eyes, and when we wander with Endymion the Moon grows amorous of our youth. Ours is the anguish of Atys, and ours the weak rage and noble sorrows of the Dane. Do you think that it is the imagination that enables us to live these countless lives? Yes; it is the imagination; and the imagination is the result of heredity. It is simply concentrated race-experience.

ERNEST: But where in this is the function of the critical spirit?

GILBERT: The culture that this transmission of racial experiences makes possible can be made perfect by the critical spirit alone, and indeed may be said to be one with it. For who is the true critic but he who bears within himself the dreams, and ideas, and feelings of myriad generations, and to whom no form of thought is alien, no emotional impulse obscure? And who the true man of culture, if not he who by fine scholarship and fastidious rejection has made instinct self-conscious and intelligent, and can separate the work that has distinction from the work that has it not, and so by contact and comparison makes himself master of the secrets of style and school, and understands their meanings, and listens to their voices, and develop that spirit of disinterested curiosity which is the real root, as it is the real flower, of the intellectual life, and thus attains to intellectual clarity, and, having learned "the best that is known and thought in the world," lives — it is not fanciful to say so — with those who are the Immortals.

Yes, Ernest: the contemplative life, the life that has for its aim not *doing* but *being*, and not *being* merely, but *becoming* — that is what the critical spirit can give us. The gods live thus: either brooding over their own perfection, as Aristotle tells us, or, as Epicurus fancied, watching with the calm eyes of the spectator the tragi-comedy of the world that they have made. We, too, might live like them, and set ourselves to witness with appropriate emotions the varied

scenes that man and nature afford. We might make ourselves spiritual by detaching ourselves from action, and become perfect by the rejection of energy. It has often
seemed to me that Browning felt something of this.
Shakespeare hurls Hamlet into active life, and makes him
realize his mission by effort. Browning might have given us
a Hamlet who would have realized his mission by thought.
Incident and event were to him unreal or unmeaning. He
made the soul the protagonist of life's tragedy, and looked
on action as the one undramatic element of a play. To us, at
any rate, the ΒΙΟΣΘΕΩΡΗΤΙΚΘΣ (life of contemplation)
is the true ideal. From the high tower of Thought we can
look out at the world. Calm, and self-centered, and complete, the æsthetic critic contemplates life, and no arrow
drawn at a venture can pierce between the joints of his har-
ness. He at least is safe. He has discovered how to live.

Is such a mode of life immoral? Yes; all the arts are immoral, except those baser forms of sensual or didactic art
that seek to excite to action of evil or of good. For action
of every kind belongs to the sphere of ethics. The aim of
art is simply to create a mood. Is such a mode of life unpractical? Ah! it is not so easy to be unpractical as the ignorant Philistine imagines. It were well for England if it were
so. There is no country in the world so much in need of
unpractical people as this country of ours. With us,
Thought is degraded by its constant association with practice. Who that moves in the stress and turmoil of actual
existence, noisy politician, or brawling social reformer, or
poor narrow-minded priest blinded by the sufferings of
that unimportant section of the community among
whom he has cast his lot, can seriously claim to be able to
form a disinterested intellectual judgment about any one

thing? Each of the professions means a prejudice. The necessity for a career forces every one to take sides. We live in the age of the overworked, and the under-educated; the age in which people are so industrious that they become absolutely stupid. And, harsh though it may sound, I cannot help saying that such people deserve their doom. The sure way of knowing nothing about life is to try to make oneself useful.

ERNEST: A charming doctrine, Gilbert.

GILBERT: I am not sure about that, but it has at least the minor merit of being true. That the desire to do good to others produces a plentiful crop of prigs is the least of the evils of which it is the cause. The prig is a very interesting psychological study, and though of all poses a moral pose is the most offensive, still to have a pose at all is something. It is a formal recognition of the importance of treating life from a definite and reasoned standpoint. That Humanitarian Sympathy wars against Nature, by securing the survival of the failure, may make the man of science loathe its facile virtues. The political economist may cry out against it for putting the improvident on the same level as the provident, and so robbing life of the strongest, because most sordid, incentive to industry. But in the eyes of the thinker, the real harm that emotional sympathy does is that it limits knowledge, and so prevents us from solving any single social problem. We are trying at present to stave off the coming crisis, the coming revolution, as my friends the Fabianists call it, by means of doles and alms. Well, when the revolution of crisis arrives, we shall be powerless, because we shall know nothing. And so, Ernest, let us not be deceived. England will never be civilized till she has added Utopia to her dominions. There is more than one of her colonies that she might with advantage surrender for so fair a land. What we want are unpractical people who see beyond the moment, and think beyond the day. Those who try to lead the people can only do so by following the mob. It is through the voice of one crying in the wilderness that the ways of the gods must be prepared.

the Monk

The largest monastic ruin in Europe can be found in the Yorkshire moors. Fountains Abbey was built by an order of Cistercian monks according to specifications that encouraged contemplation of the eternal, of that which exists outside of the now. The plain simplicity of the architecture, its subordination of form to function, ensured that the minds of the monks were not debased by follies.

It is only when you run your hands over the minimal, and much eroded, texture of the stone that you realize what it means to be secular, stuck in time, where every object changes and fluctuates and, generally, has knobs on.

And so it was with the Cistercians in mind that we decided to call the following section The Monk. Idleness is by definition an act of abstinence. It refuses to participate in the slew of the ever-present, of lifestyles and fashions ground out on the hurdy-gurdy of mainstream life. Increasingly, a walk down a nineties High Street is like being poked in the eye by a thousand advertising executives, simultaneously. We sample Zen and the pastoral dreams of hermits in the hope of defending ourselves against such attacks.

Wisdom from Lao Tzu

LAO TZU, C. 300 BC

This ancient Chinese philosopher — later alluded to by George Harrison — speaks of the world within. In other words, adventuring is not the path to understanding as knowledge can only ever come from within. Just sit down and contemplate.

He never goes outside his door,
Yet he is familiar with the whole world.
He never looks out of his window,
Yet he fathoms the Way of Heaven.
Truly, the farther one travels
The less he understands.
Therefore the Sage knows without investigating . . .
Does nothing, yet accomplishes everything.

from *Swann's Way*

MARCEL PROUST, 1913

A choice snippet from the master of the idle moment.

After leaving this park the Vivonne began to flow again more swiftly. How often have I watched, and longed to imitate when I should be free to live as I chose, a rower who had shipped his oars and lay flat on his back in the bottom of his boat, letting it drift with the current, seeing nothing but the sky gliding slowly by above him, his face aglow with a foretaste of happiness and peace!

We would sit down among the irises at the water's edge. In the holiday sky an idle cloud languorously dawdled. From time to time, oppressed by boredom, a carp would heave itself out of the water with an anxious gasp. It was time for our picnic. Before starting homewards we would sit there for a long time, eating fruit and bread and chocolate, on the grass over which came to us, faint, horizontal, but dense and metallic still, echoes of the bells of Saint-Hilaire, which had not melted into the air they had traversed for so long, and, ribbed by the successive palpitation of all their sound-waves, throbbed as they grazed the flowers at our feet.

---

from *The Importance of Loafing*
LIN YUTANG, 1938

The Chinese philosopher Lin Yutang declared of himself, "I am not deep and I am not well read."

I. Man the Only Working Animal

The feast of life is, therefore, before us, and the only question is what appetite we have for it. The appetite is the thing, and not the feast. After all, the most bewildering thing about man is his idea of work and the amount of work he imposes upon himself, or civilization has imposed upon him. All nature loafs, while man alone works for a living. He works because he has to, because with the progress of civilization life gets incredibly more complex, with duties, responsibilities, fears, inhibitions and ambitions, born not of nature, but of human society. While I am sitting here before my desk, a pigeon is flying about a church steeple before my window, not worrying what it is going to have for lunch. I know that my lunch is a more complicated affair than the pigeon's, and that the few articles of food I take involve thousands of people at work and a highly complicated system of cultivation, merchandising, transportation, delivery and preparation. That is why it is harder for man to get food than for animals. Nevertheless, if a jungle beast were let loose in a city and gained some apprehension of what busy human life was all about, he would feel a good deal of skepticism and bewilderment about this human society.

The first thought that the jungle beast would have is that man is the only working animal. With the exception of a few draught-horses or buffaloes made to work a mill, even domestic pets don't have to work. Police dogs are but rarely called upon to do their duty; a house-dog supposed to watch a house plays most of the time, and takes a good nap in the morning whenever there is good, warm sunshine; the aristocratic cat certainly never works for a living, and gifted with a bodily agility which enables it to disregard a neighbor's fence, it is even unconscious of its captivity — it just goes wherever it likes to go. So, then, we have this toiling humanity alone, caged and domesticated, *but not fed*, forced by this civilization and complex society to work and worry about the matter of feeding itself. Humanity has its own advantages, I am quite aware — the delights of knowledge, the pleasures of conversation and the joys of the imagination, as for instance in watching a stage play. But the essential fact remains that human life has got too complicated and the matter of merely feeding ourselves, directly or indirectly, is occupying well over ninety per cent of our human activities. Civilization is largely a matter of seeking food, while progress is that development which makes food more and more difficult to get. If it had not been made so difficult for man to obtain his food, there would be absolutely no reason why humanity should work so hard. The danger is that we get over-civilized and that we come to a point, as indeed we have already done, when the work of getting food is so strenuous that we lose our appetite for food in the process of getting it. This doesn't seem to make very much sense, from the point of view either of the jungle beast or the philosopher.

Every time I see a city skyline or look over a stretch of roofs, I get frightened. It is positively amazing. Two or three water towers, the backs of two or three steel frames for billboards, perhaps a spire or two, and a stretch of asphalt roofing material and bricks going up in square, sharp, vertical outlines without any form or order, sprinkled with some dirty, discolored chimneys and a few wash-lines and criss-cross lines of radio aerials. And looking down into a street, I see again a stretch of gray or discolored red-brick walls, with tiny, dark, uniform windows in uniform rows, half open and half hidden by shades, with perhaps a bottle of milk standing on a window-sill and a few pots of tiny, sickly flowers on some others. A child comes up to the roof with her dog and sits on the roof-stairs every morning to get a bit of sunshine. And as I lift my eyes again, I see rows upon rows of roofs, miles of them, stretching in ugly square outlines to the distance. More water towers, more brick houses. And humanity live here. How do they live, each family behind one or two of these dark windows? What do they do for a living? It is staggering. Behind every two or three windows, a couple go to bed every night like pigeons returning to their pigeon-holes; then they wake up and have their morning coffee and the husband emerges into the street, going somewhere to find bread for the family, while the wife tries persistently and desperately to drive out the dust and keep the little place clean. By four or five o'clock they come out on their doorsteps to chat with and look at their neighbors and get a sniff of fresh air. Then night falls, they are dead tired and go to sleep again. And so they live!

There are others, more well-to-do people, living in better apartments. More "arty" rooms and lampshades. Still more orderly and more clean! They have a little more space, but only a little more. To rent a seven-room flat, not to speak of owning it, is considered a luxury! But it does not imply more happiness. Less financial worry and fewer debts to think about, it is true. But also more emotional complications, more divorce, more cat-husbands that don't come home at night, or the couple go prowling together at night, seeking some form of dissipation. *Diversion* is the word. Good Lord, they need to be diverted from these monotonous, uniform brick walls and shining wooden floors! Of course they go to look at naked women. Consequently more neurasthenia, more aspirin, more expensive illnesses, more colitis, appendicitis and dyspepsia, more softened brains and hardened livers, more ulcerated duodenums and lacerated intestines, overworked stomachs and overtaxed kidneys, inflamed bladders and outraged spleens, dilated hearts and shattered nerves, more flat chests and high blood-pressure, more diabetes, Bright's disease, beri-beri, rheumatism, insomnia, arterio-sclerosis, piles, fistulas, chronic dysentery, chronic constipation, loss of appetite and weariness of life.

To make the picture perfect, more dogs and fewer children. The matter of happiness depends entirely upon the quality and temper of the men and women living in these elegant apartments. Some indeed have a jolly life, others simply don't. But on the whole, perhaps they are less happy than the hard-working people; they have more *ennui* and more boredom. But they have a car, and perhaps a country home. Ah, the country home, that is their salvation! So then, people work hard in the country so that they can come to the city so that they can earn sufficient money and go back to the country again.

And as you take a stroll through the city, you see that back of the main avenue with beauty parlors and flower shops and shipping firms is another street with drug stores, grocery stores, hardware shops, barber shops, laundries, cheap eating places, news-stands. You wander along for an hour, and if it is a big city, you are still there; you see only more streets, more drug stores, grocery stores, hardware shops, barber shops, laundries, cheap eating places and news-stands. How do these people make their living? And why do they come here? Very simple. The laundrymen wash the clothes of the barbers and restaurant waiters, the restaurant waiters wait upon the laundrymen and barbers while they eat, and the barbers cut the hair of the laundrymen and waiters. That is civilization. Isn't it amazing? I bet some of the laundrymen, barbers and waiters never wander beyond ten blocks from their place of work in their entire life. Thank God they have at least the movies, where they can see birds singing on the screen, trees growing and swaying. Turkey, Egypt, the Himalayas, the Andes, storms, shipwrecks, coronation ceremonies, ants, caterpillars, musk-rats, a fight between lizards and scorpions, hills, waves, sands, clouds, and even a moon — all on the screen!

O wise humanity, terribly wise humanity! Of thee I sing. How inscrutable is the civilization where men toil and work and worry their hair gray to get a living and forget to play!

II. The Chinese Theory of Leisure

The American is known as a great hustler, as the Chinese is known as a great loafer. And as all opposites admire each other, I suspect that the American hustler admires the Chinese loafer as much as the Chinese loafer admires the American hustler. Such things are called the charms of national traits. I do not know if eventually the West and the East will meet; the plain fact is that they are meeting now, and are going to meet more and more closely as modern civilization spreads, with the increase of communication facilities. At least, in China, we are not going to defy this machine civilization, and there the problem will have to be worked out as to how we are going to merge these two cultures, the ancient Chinese philosophy of life and the modern technological civilization, and integrate them into a sort of working way of life. The question is very much more problematical as to Occidental life ever being invaded by Oriental philosophy, although no one would dare to prophesy.

After all, the machine culture is rapidly bringing us nearer to the age of leisure, and man will be compelled to play more and work less. It is all a matter of environment, and when man finds leisure hanging on his hand, he will be forced to think more about the ways and means of wisely enjoying his leisure, conferred upon him, against his will, by rapidly improving methods of quick production. After all, no one can predict anything about the next century. He would be a brave man who dared even to predict about life thirty years from now. The constant rush for progress must certainly one day reach a point when man will be pretty tired of it all, and will begin to take stock of his conquests in the material world. I cannot believe that, with the coming of better material conditions of life, when diseases are eliminated, poverty is decreased and man's expectation of life is prolonged and food is plentiful, man will care to be as busy as he is today. I'm not so sure that a more lazy temperament will not arise as a result of this new environment.

Apart from all this, the subjective factor is always as important as the objective. Philosophy comes in as a way of changing man's outlook and also changing his character. How man is going to react toward this machine civilization depends on what kind of a man he is. In the realm of biology, there are such things as sensibility to stimulus, slowness or quickness of reaction, and different behaviors of different animals in the same medium or environment. Some animals react more slowly than others. Even in this machine civilization, which I understand includes the United States, England, France, Germany, Italy and Russia, we see that different reactions toward the mechanical age arise from different racial temperaments. The chances of peculiar individual reactions to the same environment are not eliminated. For China, I feel the type of life resulting from it will be very much like that in modern France, because the Chinese and the French temperaments are so akin.

America today is most advanced in machine civilization, and it has always been assumed that the future of a world dominated by the machine will tend toward the present American type and pattern of life. I feel inclined to dispute this thesis, because no one knows yet what the American temperament is going to be. At best we can only describe it as a changing temperament. I do not think it at all impossible that there may be a revival of that period of New England culture so well described in Van Wyck Brooks's new book. No one can say that that flowering of New England culture was not typically American culture, and certainly no one can say that that ideal Walt Whitman envisaged in his *Democratic Vistas*, pointing to the development of free men and perfect mothers, is not the ideal of democratic progress. America needs only to be given a little respite, and there may be — I am quite sure there will be — new Whitmans, new Thoreaus and new Lowells, when that old American culture, cut short literally and figuratively by the gold rush, may blossom forth again. Will not, then, American temperament be something quite different from that of the present day, and very near to the temperament of Emerson and Thoreau?

Culture, as I understand it, is essentially a product of leisure. The art of culture is therefore essentially the art of loafing. From the Chinese point of view, the man who is wisely idle is the most cultured man. For there seems to be a philosophic contradiction between being busy and being wise. Those who are wise won't be busy, and those who are too busy can't be wise. The wisest man is therefore he who loafs most gracefully. Here I shall try to explain, not the technique and varieties of loafing as practiced in China, but rather the philosophy which nourishes this divine desire for loafing in China and gives rise to that carefree, idle, happy-go-lucky — and often poetic — temperament in the Chinese scholars, and to a lesser extent, in the Chinese people in general. How did that Chinese temperament — that distrust of achievement and success and that intense love of living as such — arise?

In the first place, the Chinese theory of leisure, as expressed by a comparatively unknown author of the eighteenth century, Shu Paihsiang, who happily achieved oblivion, is as follows: time is useful because it is not being used. "Leisure in time is like unoccupied floor space in a room." Every working girl who rents a small room where every inch of space is fully utilized feels highly uncomfortable because she has no room to move about, and the moment she gets a rise in salary, she moves into a bigger room where there is a little more unused floor space, besides those strictly useful spaces occupied by her single bed, her dressing table and her two-burner gas range. It is that unoccupied space which makes a room habitable, as it is our leisure hours which make life endurable. I understand there is a rich woman living on Park Avenue who bought up a neighboring lot to prevent anybody from erecting a skyscraper next to her house. She is paying a big sum of money in order to have space fully and perfectly made useless, and it seems to me she never spent her money more wisely.

In this connection, I might mention a personal experience. I could never see the beauty of skyscrapers in New York, and it was not until I went to Chicago that I realized that a skyscraper could be very imposing and very beautiful to look at, if it had a good frontage and at least half a mile of unused space around it. Chicago is fortunate in this respect, because it has more space than Manhattan. The tall buildings are better spaced, and there is the possibility of obtaining an unobstructed view of them from a long distance. Figuratively speaking, we, too, are so cramped in our life that we cannot enjoy a free perspective of the beauties of our spiritual life. We lack spiritual frontage.

III. *The Cult of the Idle Life*

*T*he Chinese love of leisure arises from a combination of causes. It came from a temperament, was erected into a literary cult, and found its justification in a philosophy. It grew out of an intense love of life, was actively sustained by an underlying current of literary romanticism throughout the dynasties, and was eventually pronounced right and sensible by a philosophy of life, which we may, in the main, describe as Taoistic. The rather general acceptance of this Taoistic view of life is only proof that there is Taoistic blood in the Chinese temperament.

And here we must first clarify one point. The romantic cult of the idle life, which we have defined as a product of leisure, was decidedly not for the wealthy class, as we usually understand it to be. That would be an unmitigated error in the approach to the problem. It was a cult for the poor and unsuccessful and humble scholar who either had chosen the idle life or had idleness enforced upon him. As I read Chinese literary masterpieces, and as I imagine the poor schoolmaster teaching the poor scholars these poems and essays glorifying the simple and idle life, I cannot help thinking that they must have derived an immense personal satisfaction and spiritual consolation from them. Disquisitions on the handicaps of fame and advantages of obscurity sounded pleasing to those who had failed in the civil examinations, and such sayings as "Eating late (with appetite whetted) is eating meat" tended to make the bad provider less apologetic to his family. No greater misjudgment of literary history is made than when the young Chinese proletarian writers accuse the poets Su Tungp'o and T'ao Yüanming and others of belonging to the hated leisure-class intelligentsia — Su who sang about "the clear breeze over the stream and bright moon over the hills," and T'ao who sang about "the dew making wet his skirt" and "a hen roosting on the top of a mulberry tree." As if the river breeze and the moon over the hills and the hen roosting on a mulberry tree were owned only by the capitalist class! These great men of the past went beyond the stage of talking about peasant conditions, and lived the life of the poor peasant themselves and found peace and harmony in it.

In this sense I regard this romantic cult of the idle life as essentially democratic. We can better understand this romantic cult when we picture for ourselves Laurence Sterne on his sentimental journey, or Wordsworth and Coleridge hiking through Europe on foot with a great sense of beauty in their breast but very little money in their purse. There was a time when one didn't have to be rich in order to travel, and even to-day travel doesn't have to be a luxury of the rich. On the whole, the enjoyment of leisure is something which decidedly costs less than the enjoyment of luxury. All it requires is an artistic temperament which is bent on seeking a perfectly useless afternoon spent in a perfectly useless manner. The idle life really costs so very little, as Thoreau took the trouble to point out in *Walden*.

The Chinese romanticists were, on the whole, men gifted with a high sensibility and a vagabond nature, poor in their worldly possessions, but rich in sentiment. They had an intense love of life which showed itself in their abhorrence of all official life and a stern refusal to make the soul serf to the body. The idle life, so far from being the prerogative of the rich and powerful and successful (how busy the successful American men are!), was in China an achievement of *high-mindedness*, a high-mindedness very near to the Western conception of the dignity of the tramp who is too proud to ask favors, too independent to go to work, and too wise to take the world's successes too seriously. This high-mindedness came from, and was inevitably associated with, a certain sense of *detachment* toward the drama of life; it came from the quality of being able to see through life's ambitions and follies and the temptations of fame and wealth. Somehow the high-minded scholar who valued his character more than his achievements, his soul more than fame or wealth, became by common consent the highest ideal of Chinese literature. Inevitably he was a man with great simplicity of living and a proud contempt for worldly success as the world understands it.

Great men of letters of this class — T'ao Yüanming, Su Tungp'o, Po Chüyi, Yüan Chunglang, Yüan Tsets'ai — were generally enticed into a short term of official life, did a wonderful job of it, and then got exasperated with its eternal kowtowing and receiving and sending off of fellow-officials, and gladly laying down the burdens of an official life, returned wisely to the life of retirement. Yüan Chunglang wrote seven successive petitions to his superior, when he was magistrate of Soochow, complaining of these eternal kowtowings, and begging to be allowed to return to the life of the free and careless individual.

A rather extravagant example of the praise of idleness is found in the inscription of another poet, Po Yüchien, written for his studio, which he called "The Hall of Idleness":

> I'm too lazy to read the Taoist classics, for *Tao* doesn't reside in the books;
> Too lazy to look over the sutras, for they go no deeper in *Tao* than its looks.
> The essence of *Tao* consists in a void, clear, and cool,
> But what is this void except being the whole day like a fool?
> Too lazy am I to read poetry, for when I stop, the poetry will be gone;
> Too lazy to play on the *ch'in*, for music dies on the string where it's born;
> Too lazy to drink wine, for beyond the drunkard's dream there are rivers and lakes;
> Too lazy to play chess, for besides the pawns there are other stakes;
> Too lazy to look at the hills and streams, for there is a painting within my heart's portals;
> Too lazy to face the wind and the moon, for within me is the Isle of the Immortals;
> Too lazy to attend to worldly affairs, for inside me are my hut and my possessions;

Too lazy to watch the changing of the seasons, for
within me are heavenly processions.

Pine trees may decay and rocks may rot; but I shall
always remain what I am.

Is it not fitting that I call this the Hall of Idleness?

This cult of idleness was therefore always bound up
with a life of inner calm, a sense of carefree irresponsibility
and an intense wholehearted enjoyment of the life of nature. Poets and scholars have always given themselves
quaint names, like "The Guest of Rivers and Lakes" (Tu
Fu); "The Recluse of the Eastern Hillside" (Su Tungp'o);
the "Carefree Man of a Misty Lake"; and "The Old Man of
the Haze-girdled Tower," etc.

No, the enjoyment of an idle life doesn't cost any
money. The capacity for true enjoyment of idleness is lost
in the moneyed class and can be found only among people who have a supreme contempt for wealth. It must
come from an inner richness of the soul in a man who
loves the simple ways of life and who is somewhat impatient with the business of making money. There is always
plenty of life to enjoy for a man who is determined to enjoy it. If men fail to enjoy this earthly existence we have,
it is because they do not love life sufficiently and allow it
to be turned into a humdrum routine existence. Laotse
has been wrongly accused of being hostile to life; on the
other hand, I think he taught the renunciation of the life
of the world exactly because he loved life all too tenderly,
to allow the art of living to degenerate into a mere business of living.

For where there is love, there is jealousy; a man who
loves life intensely must be always jealous of the few exqui-

site moments of leisure that he has. And he must retain the dignity and pride always characteristic of a vagabond. His hours of fishing must be as sacred as his hours of business, erected into a kind of religion as the English have done with sport. He must be as impatient at having people talk to him about the stock market at the golf club, as the scientist is at having anybody disturb him in his laboratory. And he must count the days of departing spring with a sense of sad regret for not having made more trips or excursions, as a business man feels when he has not sold so many wares in the day.

VI. *Three American Vices*

To the Chinese, therefore, with the fine philosophy that "Nothing matters to a man who says nothing matters," Americans offer a strange contrast. Is life really worth all the bother, to the extent of making our soul a slave to the body? The high spirituality of the philosophy of loafing forbids it. The most characteristic advertisement I ever saw was one by an engineering firm with the big words: "Nearly Right Is Not Enough." The desire for one hundred per cent efficiency seems almost obscene. The trouble with Americans is that when a thing is nearly right, they want to make it still better, while for a Chinese, nearly right is good enough.

The three great American vices seem to be efficiency, punctuality and the desire for achievements and success. They are the things that make the Americans so unhappy and so nervous. They steal from them their inalienable right of loafing and cheat them of many a good, idle and beautiful afternoon. One must start out with a belief that there are no catastrophes in this world, and that, besides the noble art of getting things done, there is a nobler art of leaving things undone. On the whole, if one answers letters promptly, the result is about as good or as bad as if he had never answered them at all. After all, nothing happens, and while one may have missed a few good appointments, one may have also avoided a few unpleasant ones. Most of the letters are not worth answering, if you keep them in your drawer for three months; reading them three months afterwards, one might realize how utterly futile and what a waste of time it would have been to answer them all. Writing letters really can become a vice. It turns our writers into fine promotion salesmen and our college professors into good efficient business executives. In this sense, I can understand Thoreau's contempt for the American who always goes to the post office.

Our quarrel is not that efficiency gets things done and very well done, too. I always rely on American water-taps, rather than on those made in China, because American water-taps do not leak. That is a consolation. Against the old contention, however, that we must all be useful, be efficient, become officials and have power, the old reply is that there are always enough fools in the world who are willing to be useful, be busy and enjoy power, and so somehow the business of life can and will be carried on. The only point is who are the wise, the loafers or the hustlers? Our quarrel with efficiency is not that it gets things done, but that it is a thief of time when it leaves us no leisure to enjoy ourselves and that it frays our nerves in trying to get things done perfectly. An American editor worries his hair gray to see that no typographical mistakes appear on the pages of his magazine. The Chinese editor is wiser than that. He wants to leave his readers the supreme satisfaction of discovering a few typographical mistakes for themselves. More than that, a Chinese magazine can begin printing serial fiction and forget about it half-way. In America it might bring the roof down on the editors, but in China *it doesn't matter, simply because it doesn't matter*. American engineers in building bridges calculate so finely and exactly as to make the two ends come together within one-tenth of an inch. But when two Chinese begin to dig a tunnel from both sides of a mountain, both come out on the other side. The Chinese's firm conviction is that it doesn't matter so long as a tunnel is dug through, and if we have two instead of one, why, we have a double track to boot. Provided you are not in a hurry, two tunnels are as good as one, dug somehow, finished somehow and if the train can get through somehow. And the Chinese are extremely punctual, provided you give them plenty of time to do a thing. They always finish a thing on schedule, provided the schedule is long enough.

The tempo of modern industrial life forbids this kind of glorious and magnificent idling. But worse than that, it imposes upon us a different conception of time as measured by the clock, and eventually turns the human being into a clock himself. This sort of thing is bound to come to China, as is evident, for instance, in a factory of twenty thousand workers. The luxurious prospect of twenty thousand workers coming in at their own sweet pleasure at all hours is, of course, somewhat terrifying. Nevertheless, this is what makes life so hard and hectic. A man who has to be punctually at a certain place at five o'clock has the whole afternoon from one to five ruined for him already. Every American adult is arranging his time on the pattern of the schoolboy — three o'clock for this, five o'clock for that, six-thirty for change of dress; six-fifty for entering the taxi and seven o'clock for emerging into a hotel room. It just makes life not worth living.

And Americans have now come to such a sad state that they are booked up not only for the following day, or the following week, but even for the following month. An appointment three weeks ahead of time is a thing unknown in China. And when a Chinese receives an invitation card, happily he never has to say whether he is going to be present or not. He can put down on the invitation list "Coming" if he accepts, or "Thanks" if he declines, but in the majority of cases the invited party merely writes the word "Know," which is a statement of fact that he knows of the invitation and not a statement of intention. An American or a European leaving Shanghai can tell me that he is going to attend a committee meeting in Paris on April 19, 1938, at three o'clock and that he will be arriving in Vienna on May 21st by the seven o'clock train. If an afternoon is to be condemned and executed, must we announce its execution so early? Cannot a fellow travel and be lord of himself, arriving when he likes and taking departure when he likes?

But above all, the American's inability to loaf comes directly from his desire for doing things and in his placing action above being. We should demand that there be character in our lives as we demand there be character in all great art worthy of the name. Unfortunately, character is not a thing which can be manufactured overnight. Like the quality of mellowness in wine, it is acquired by standing still and by the passage of time. The desire of American old men and women for action, trying in this way to gain their self-respect and the respect of the younger generation, is what makes them look so ridiculous to an Oriental. Too much action in an old man is like a broadcast of jazz music from a megaphone on top of an old cathedral. Is it not sufficient that the old people *are* something? Is it necessary that they must be for ever *doing* something? The loss of the capacity for loafing is bad enough in men of middle age, but the same loss in old age is a crime committed against human nature.

Character is always associated with something old and takes time to grow, like the beautiful facial lines of a man in middle age, lines that are the steady imprint of the man's evolving character. It is somewhat difficult to see character in a type of life where every man is throwing away his last year's car and trading it in for the new model. As are the things we make, so are we ourselves. In 1937 every man and woman look 1937, and in 1938 every man and woman will look 1938. We love old cathedrals, old furniture, old silver, old dictionaries and old prints, but we have entirely forgotten about the beauty of old men. I think an appreciation of that kind of beauty is essential to our life, for beauty, it seems to me, is what is old and mellow and well-smoked.

Sometimes a prophetic vision comes to me, a beautiful vision of a millennium when Manhattan will go slow, and when the American "go-getter" will become an Oriental loafer. American gentlemen will float in skirts and slippers and amble on the sidewalks of Broadway with their hands in their pockets, if not with both hands stuck in their sleeves in the Chinese fashion. Policemen will exchange a word of greeting with the slow-devil at the crossings, and the drivers themselves will stop and accost each other and inquire after their grandmothers' health in the midst of traffic. Someone will be brushing his teeth outside his shop-front, talking the while placidly with his neighbors, and once in a while, an absent-minded scholar will sail by with a limp volume rolled up and tucked away in his sleeve. Lunch counters will be abolished, and people will be lolling and lounging in soft, low armchairs in an Automat, while others will have learned the art of killing a whole afternoon in some café. A glass of orange juice will last half an hour, and people will learn to sip wine by slow mouthfuls, punctuated by delightful, chatty remarks, instead of swallowing it at a gulp. Registration in a hospital will be abolished, "emergency wards" will be unknown, and patients will exchange their philosophy with their doctors. Fire engines will proceed at a snail's pace, their staff stopping on the way to gaze at and dispute over the number of passing wild geese in the sky. It is too bad that there is no hope of this kind of a millennium on Manhattan ever being realized. There might be so many more perfect idle afternoons.

---

from *Pensées*

PASCAL, 1670

Blaise Pascal was an internationally renowned mathematician and philosopher who defined the human condition as "inconstancy, boredom, anxiety." In the following extract, he describes how activity helps to numb overworked minds.

Sometimes, when I set to thinking about the various activities of men, the dangers and troubles which they face at Court, or in war, giving rise to so many quarrels and passions, daring and often wicked enterprises and so on, I have often said that the sole cause of man's unhappiness is that he does not know how to stay quietly in his room. A man wealthy enough for life's needs would never leave home to go to sea or besiege some fortress if he knew how to stay at home and enjoy it. Men would never spend so much on a commission in the army if they could bear living in town all their lives, and they only seek after the company and diversion of gambling because they do not enjoy staying at home.

But after closer thought, looking for the particular reasons for all our unhappiness now that I knew its general cause, I found one very cogent reason in the natural unhappiness of our feeble mortal condition, so wretched that nothing can console us when we really think about it.

Imagine any situation you like, add up all the blessings with which you could be endowed, to be king is still the finest thing in the world; yet if you imagine one with all the advantages of his rank, but no means of diversion, left to ponder and reflect on what he is, this limp felicity will not keep him going; he is bound to start thinking of all the threats facing him, of possible revolts, finally of inescapable death and disease, with the result that if he is deprived of so-called diversion he is unhappy, indeed more unhappy than the humblest of his subjects who can enjoy sport and diversion.

The only good thing for men therefore is to be diverted from thinking of what they are, either by some occupation which takes their mind off it, or by some novel and agreeable passion which keeps them busy, like gambling, hunting, some absorbing show, in short by what is called diversion.

That is why gaming and feminine society, war and high office are so popular. It is not that they really bring happiness, nor that anyone imagines that true bliss comes from possessing the money to be won at gaming or the hare that is hunted: no one would take it as a gift. What people want is not the easy peaceful life that allows us to think of our unhappy condition, nor the dangers of war, nor the burdens of office, but the agitation that takes our mind off it and diverts us. That is why we prefer the hunt to the capture.

That is why men are so fond of hustle and bustle; that is why prison is such a fearful punishment; that is why the pleasures of solitude are so incomprehensible. That, in fact, is the main joy of being a king, because people are continually trying to divert him and procure him every kind of pleasure. A king is surrounded by people whose only thought is to divert him and stop him thinking about himself, because, king though he is, he becomes unhappy as soon as he thinks about himself.

That is all that men have been able to devise for attaining happiness; those who philosophize about it, holding that people are quite unreasonable to spend all day chasing a hare that they would not have wanted to buy, have little knowledge of our nature. The hare itself would not save us from thinking about death and the miseries distracting us, but hunting it does so. Thus when Pyrrhus was advised to take the rest towards which he was so strenuously striving, he found it very hard to do so.

Telling a man to rest is the same as telling him to live

happily. It means advising him to enjoy a completely happy state which he can contemplate at leisure without cause for distress. It means not understanding nature.

Thus men who are naturally conscious of what they are shun nothing so much as rest; they would do anything to be disturbed.

It is wrong then to blame them; they are not wrong to want excitement — if they only wanted it for the sake of diversion. The trouble is that they want it as though, once they had the things they seek, they could not fail to be truly happy. That is what justifies calling their search a vain one. All this shows that neither the critics nor the criticized understand man's real nature.

When men are reproached for pursuing so eagerly something that could never satisfy them, their proper answer, if they really thought about it, ought to be that they simply want a violent and vigorous occupation to take their minds off themselves, and that is why they choose some attractive object to entice them in ardent pursuit. Their opponents could find no answer to that,

(Vanity, pleasure of showing off. Dancing, you must think where to put your feet.)

but they do not answer like that because they do not know themselves. They do not know that all they want is the hunt and not the capture. The nobleman sincerely believes that hunting is a great sport, the sport of kings, but his huntsman does not feel like that. They imagine that if they secured a certain appointment they would enjoy resting afterwards, and they do not realize the insatiable nature of cupidity. They think they genuinely want rest when all they really want is activity.

They have a secret instinct driving them to seek external diversion and occupation, and this is the result of their constant sense of wretchedness. They have another secret instinct, left over from the greatness of our original nature, telling them that the only true happiness lies in rest and not in excitement. These two contrary instincts give rise to a confused plan buried out of sight in the depths of their soul, which leads them to seek rest by way of activity and always to imagine that the satisfaction they miss will come to them once they overcome certain obvious difficulties and can open the door to welcome rest.

All our life passes in this way: we seek rest by struggling against certain obstacles, and once they are overcome, rest proves intolerable because of the boredom it produces. We must get away from it and crave excitement.

We think either of present or of threatened miseries, and even if we felt quite safe on every side, boredom on its own account would not fail to emerge from the depths of our hearts, where it is naturally rooted, and poison our whole mind.

Man is so unhappy that he would be bored even if he had no cause for boredom, by the very nature of his temperament, and he is so vain that, though he has a thousand and one basic reasons for being bored, the slightest thing, like pushing a ball with a billiard cue, will be enough to divert him.

"But," you will say, "what is his object in all this?" Just so that he can boast tomorrow to his friends that he played better than someone else. Likewise others sweat away in their studies to prove to scholars that they have solved some hitherto insoluble problem in algebra. Many others again, just as foolishly in my view, risk the greatest dangers so that they can boast afterwards of having captured some stronghold. Then there are others who exhaust themselves observing all these things, not in order to become wiser, but just to show they know them, and these are the biggest fools of the lot, because they know what they are doing, while it is conceivable that the rest would stop being foolish if they knew too.

Ode on Indolence

JOHN KEATS, 1819

Keats, as a romantic, could not remain untouched by the ideal of eternal indolence. But could he resist the siren strains of Love, Ambition and Poesy?

They toil not, neither do they spin

I

One morn before me were three figures seen,
With bowèd necks, and joinèd hands, side-faced;
And one behind the other stepped serene,
In placid sandals, and in white robes graced;
They passed, like figures on a marble urn,
When shifted round to see the other side;
They came again; as when the urn once more
Is shifted round, the first seen shades return;
And they were strange to me, as may betide
With vases, to one deep in Phidian lore.

II

How is it, Shadows! that I knew ye not?
How came ye muffled in so hush a masque?
Was it a silent deep-disguisèd plot
To steal away, and leave without a task
My idle days? Ripe was the drowsy hour;
The blissful cloud of summer-indolence
Benumbed my eyes; my pulse grew less and less;
Pain had no sting, and pleasure's wreath no flower:
O, why did ye not melt, and leave my sense
Unhaunted quite of all but – nothingness?

III

A third time passed they by, and, passing, turned
Each one the face a moment whiles to me;
Then faded, and to follow them I burned
And ached for wings because I knew the three;
The first was a fair Maid, and Love her name;
The second was Ambition, pale of cheek,
And ever watchful with fatiguèd eye;
The last, whom I love more, the more of blame
Is heaped upon her, maiden most unmeek –
I knew to be my demon Poesy.

IV

They faded, and, forsooth! I wanted wings.
O folly! What is love! and where is it?
And, for that poor Ambition – it springs
From a man's little heart's short fever-fit.
For Poesy! – no, she has not a joy –

At least for me — so sweet as drowsy noons,
And evenings steeped in honeyed indolence.
O, for an age so sheltered from annoy,
That I may never know how change the moons,
Or hear the voice of busy common-sense!

V

A third time came they by — alas! wherefore?
My sleep had been embroidered with dim dreams:
My soul had been a lawn besprinkled o'er
With flowers, and stirring shades, and baffled beams:
The morn was clouded, but no shower fell,
Though in her lids hung the sweet tears of May;
The open casement pressed a new-leaved vine,
Let in the budding warmth and throstle's lay;
O Shadows! 'twas a time to bid farewell!
Upon your skirts had fallen no tears of mine.

VI

So, ye three Ghosts, adieu! Ye cannot raise
My head cool-bedded in the flowery grass;
For I would not be dieted with praise,
A pet-lamb in a sentimental farce!
Fade softly from my eyes, and be once more
In masque-like figures on the dreamy urn.
Farewell! I yet have visions for the night,
And for the day faint visions there is store.
Vanish, ye Phantoms! from my idle sprite,
Into the clouds, and never more return!

from *Opium*

JEAN COCTEAU, 1930

Cocteau's account of his cure for opium addiction ranks as a classic of drug literature.

I remember at the age of eighteen or nineteen (the time of *Le Cap*) being filled with anguish at certain images. I said to myself, for example: "I am going to die and I shall not have conveyed the swallow's cries," or "I shall die without having explained the setting of empty cities at night." The Seine, the posters, tar in April, the river steamers – I took no pleasure in all these wonders. I only experienced the anguish of living too short a time to tell of them.

Having told these things, I experienced a great sense of relief. I observed with detachment. After the war the things that I hoped to say were of an increasingly uncommon kind, limited to a very few. No one could take them from me or anticipate me. I drew breath like a runner who turns round, lies down, recovers his composure and does not even see the silhouettes of the others on the horizon any more.

---

from *Provoked Life,* an Essay on the Anthropology of the Ego

GOTTFRIED BENN, 1949

The German lyric poet and physician wrote against society's trend towards the over-rational and intellectual. Here he writes approvingly of Ecuadorian drug rituals which suppress the ego.

The ingestion takes place in the rancho of dreamers in Ecuador, in tents, while the medicine man beats the drums, or in empty cellars lined with stone projections used as seats by the guests, sometimes with the women, sometimes without: the "black drink," the "white water," the "happiness pills," or the "weed of graves," which brings unity with the spirits. Stages of excitement, stages of dream — you are beside yourself, but you feel, you learn from twitches and breathing disturbances, you get apathy or mobility as desired. From hidden centers, from the depths it emerges: to rest, to move no more: withdrawal, regression, aphasia. Hours are filled with the satisfaction of the desire to drift along as formless life. To call this animalistic is to be mistaken: this process is far below the animals, below the reflexes, it is near roots, chalk and stone. This is not the apathy of a dying race, not degeneration, these are youthful people; it is something more primary: defense against the beginnings of consciousness, its senseless imperative projects — thus, change space, obliterate time, blow away the grim passage of hours.

---

from *The Marriage of Heaven and Hell*
WILLIAM BLAKE, 1792

Blake could never be accused of lucidity. However, his Proverbs of Hell *hint at meanings hidden in the squall of his longer works. The short poem* To God *is taken from Blake's notebooks.*

The hours of folly are measur'd by the clock,
but of wisdom: no clock can measure.

In seed time learn, in harvest teach, in winter enjoy.

To God

If you have found a circle to go into
Go into it yourself & see how you would do

———

from *On Experience*

MICHEL DE MONTAIGNE, 1580

Where the Renaissance thinker concludes that living well is the greatest act we can perform.

When I dance, I dance; when I sleep, I sleep: Yes, and when I am walking by myself in a beautiful orchard, even if my thoughts dwell for a time on distant events, I bring them back for another part to the walk, the orchard, the charm of this solitude, and to myself. Nature has with maternal care provided that the actions she has enjoined on us for our need shall give us pleasure; and she uses not only reason but appetite to attract us to them. It is wrong to infringe her rules. When I see Caesar and Alexander, in the thick of their greatest labors, so fully enjoying those pleasures which are natural, and therefore right and necessary, I do not say they are relaxing their minds. I say that they are bracing them, subordinating their strenuous activities and burdensome thoughts, by strength of the spirit, to the usages of everyday life. How wise they would be, if they had believed this to be their ordinary vocation and the other an extraordinary one!

We are great fools. "He has spent his life in idleness," we say, and "I have done nothing today." What! have you not lived? That is not only the fundamental, but the most noble of your occupations. "If I had been put in charge of some great affair, I might have shown what I can do." Have you been able to reflect on your life and control it? Then you have performed the greatest work of all. To reveal herself and do her work, nature has no need of fortune. She manifests herself equally at all levels, and behind curtains as well as in the open. Our duty is to compose our character, not to compose books, to win battles and provinces, but order and tranquillity in our conduct. Our great and glorious masterpiece is to live properly. All other things — to reign, to lay up treasure, to build — are at the best but little aids and additions.

---

from *Ethics*

ARISTOTLE, 330 BC

Leisure, for the Greeks, was the highest state. Work was so unpleasant to them that they developed a slave culture. Here is Aristotle on the art of contemplation.

Happiness and contemplation

If happiness is an activity in accordance with virtue, it is reasonable to assume that it is in accordance with the highest virtue, and this will be the virtue of the best part of us. Whether this is the intellect or something else that we regard as naturally ruling and guiding us, and possessing insight into things noble and divine — either as being actually divine itself or as being more divine than any other part of us — it is the activity of this part, in accordance with the virtue proper to it, that will be perfect happiness.

We have already said that it is a contemplative activity. This may be regarded as consonant both with our earlier arguments and with the truth. For contemplation is both the highest form of activity (since the intellect is the highest thing in us, and the objects that it apprehends are the highest things that can be known), and also it is the most continuous, because we are more capable of continuous contemplation than we are of any practical activity. Also we assume that happiness must contain an admixture of pleasure; now activity in accordance with [philosophic] wisdom is admittedly the most pleasant of the virtuous activities; at any rate philosophy is held to entail pleasures that are marvelous in purity and permanence; and it stands to reason that those who possess knowledge pass their time more pleasantly than those who are still in pursuit of it. Again, the quality that we call self-sufficiency will belong in the highest degree to the contemplative activity. The wise man, no less than the just one and all the rest, requires the necessaries of life; but, given an adequate supply of these, the just man also needs people with and towards whom he can perform just actions, and similarly with the temperate man, the brave man, and each of the others; but the wise man can practice contemplation by himself, and the wiser he is, the more he can do it. No doubt he does it better with the help of fellow-workers; but for all that he is the most self-sufficient of men. Again, contemplation would seem to be the only activity that is appreciated for its own sake; because nothing is gained from it except the act of contemplation, whereas from practical activities we expect to gain something more or less over and above the action.

Since happiness is thought to imply leisure,
it must be an intellectual, not a practical activity.

Also it is commonly believed that happiness depends on leisure; because we occupy ourselves so that we may have leisure, just as we make war in order that we may live at peace. Now the exercise of the practical virtues takes place in politics or in warfare, and these professions seem to have no place for leisure. This is certainly true of the military profession, for nobody chooses to make war or provokes it for the sake of making war; a man would be regarded as a bloodthirsty monster if he made his friends into enemies in order to bring about battles and slaughter. The politician's profession also makes leisure impossible, since besides the business of politics it aims at securing positions of power and honor, or the happiness of the politician himself and of his fellow-citizens – a happiness separate from politics, and one which we clearly pursue as separate.

If, then, politics and warfare, although pre-eminent in nobility and grandeur among practical activities in accordance with goodness, are incompatible with leisure and, not being desirable in themselves, are directed towards some other end, whereas the activity of the intellect is considered to excel in seriousness, taking as it does the form of contemplation, and to aim at no other end beyond itself, and to possess a pleasure peculiar to itself, which intensifies its activity; and if it is evident that self-sufficiency and leisuredness and such freedom from fatigue as is humanly possible, together with all the other attributes assigned to the supremely happy man, are those that accord with this activity; then this activity will be the perfect happiness for man – provided that it is allowed a full span of life; for nothing that pertains to happiness is incomplete.

The view that happiness is contemplation is confirmed by other arguments.

That perfect happiness is a kind of contemplative activity may be shown also from the following argument. The gods in our conception of them are supremely happy and blessed, but what kind of actions should we attribute to them? If we say "Just actions," surely we shall be confronted by the absurdity of their making contracts and returning deposits and all that sort of thing. Well, shall we say "Brave actions" — facing terrors and risking their persons in the cause of honor? What of liberal actions? They will have nobody to give to; and it is absurd that they should actually have coined money or its equivalent. What form could their temperate actions take? Surely it would be cheap praise, since they have no evil desires! If we went through the whole list we should find that the practical details of these actions are petty and unworthy of gods. On the other hand men have always conceived of them as at least living beings, and therefore active, for we cannot suppose that they spend their time in sleeping, like Endymion. But if a living being is deprived of action, and still further of production, what is left but contemplation? It follows, then, that the activity of God, which is supremely happy, must be a form of contemplation; and therefore among human activities that which is most akin to God's will be the happiest.

This view is further supported by the fact that the lower animals have no share in happiness, being completely incapable of such an activity. The life of the gods is altogether happy, and that of man is happy in so far as it contains something that resembles the divine activity; but none of the lower animals is happy, because they have no way of participating in contemplation. Happiness, then, is co-extensive with contemplation, and the more people contemplate, the happier they are; not incidentally, but in virtue of their contemplation, because it is in itself precious. Thus happiness is a form of contemplation.

But its possessor, being only human, will also need external felicity, because human nature is not self-sufficient for the purpose of contemplation; the body too must be healthy, and food and other amenities must be available. On the other hand it must not be supposed that, because one cannot be happy without external goods, it will be necessary to have many of them on a grand scale in order to be happy at all. For self-sufficiency does not depend upon a superfluity of means, nor does conduct; and it is possible to perform fine acts even if one is not master of land and sea. Indeed, a man can conduct himself virtuously even from a modest competence (this can be quite plainly seen, for private persons are considered to perform decent actions not less but actually more than those who are in positions of power). It is enough, then, to possess this much; for a man's life will be happy if he acts in accordance with virtue. Solon, too, was presumably right in his description of happy people when he said that they were those who were moderately equipped with external goods, and had achieved what were, as he thought, the finest deeds, and had lived temperate lives; for it is possible for those who have only moderate possessions to do what is right. Anaxagoras, too, seems not to have pictured the happy man as wealthy or powerful when he said that it would not surprise him if such a person were an oddity in most people's eyes, because they judge by outward appearances, which are all that they can perceive. Thus it appears that our arguments are in harmony with the opinions of the wise. Such considerations do indeed carry some conviction; but in the matter of conduct truth is assessed in the light of the facts and of actual life; because it is in these that the decisive factor lies. So we must bring what we have already said to the test of the facts of life; and if it accords with the facts, we can accept it, but if it conflicts with them we must regard it as no more than a theory.

The man who exercises his intellect and cultivates it seems likely to be in the best state of mind and to be most loved by the gods. For if, as is generally supposed, the gods have some concern for human affairs, it would be reasonable to believe also that they take pleasure in that part of us which is best and most closely related to themselves (this being the intellect), and that they reward those who appreciate and honor it most highly; for they care for what is dear to them, and what they do is right and good. Now it is not hard to see that it is the wise man that possesses these qualities in the highest degree; therefore he is dearest to the gods. And it is natural that he should also be the happiest of men. So on this score too the wise man will be happy in the highest degree.

---

from *Pensées*

PASCAL, 1670

Where the wise man admits a wise expedient: he got friends to do his reading for him.

People ask if I have myself read all the books I quote. — I reply that I have not; it would certainly have meant spending my life reading very bad books; but I read Escobar right through twice; and, as for the others, I got my friends to read them, but I did not use a single passage without reading it myself in the book quoted, going into the context involved, and reading the passage before and after it, to avoid all risk of quoting an objection as an answer, which would have been reprehensible and unjust.

---

from *Walden*
HENRY DAVID THOREAU, 1854

Thoreau was an early opponent of American materialism: in 1845 he retired to a log cabin to live a life of solitude. Later he was jailed for non-payment of poll tax. In Walden *he discusses his distaste for the life of property and excessive toil.*

I see young men, my townsmen, whose misfortune it is to have inherited farms, houses, barns, cattle, and farming tools; for these are more easily acquired than got rid of. Better if they had been born in the open pasture and suckled by a wolf, that they might have seen with clearer eyes what field they were called to labor in. Who made them serfs of the soil? Why should they eat their sixty acres, when man is condemned to eat only his peck of dirt? Why should they begin digging their graves as soon as they are born? They have got to live a man's life, pushing all these things before them, and get on as well as they can. How many a poor immortal soul have I met well nigh crushed and smothered under its load, creeping down the road of life, pushing before it a barn seventy-five feet by forty, its Augean stables never cleansed, and one hundred acres of land, tillage, mowing, pasture, and wood-lot! The portionless, who struggle with no such unnecessary inherited encumbrances, find it labor enough to subdue and cultivate a few cubic feet of flesh.

But men labor under a mistake. The better part of the man is soon ploughed into the soil for compost. By a seeming fate, commonly called necessity, they are employed, as it says in an old book, laying up treasures which moth and rust will corrupt and thieves break through and steal. It is a fool's life, as they will find when they get to the end of it, if not before. It is said that Deucalion and Pyrrha created men by throwing stones over their heads behind them:

> Inde genus durum sumus, experiensque laborum,
> Et documenta damus quâ simus origine nati.

Or, as Raleigh rhymes it in his sonorous way,

> "From thence our kind hard-hearted is, enduring pain
> and care,
> Approving that our bodies of a stony nature are."

So much for a blind obedience to a blundering oracle, throwing the stones over their heads behind them, and not seeing where they fell.

Most men, even in this comparatively free country, through mere ignorance and mistake, are so occupied with the factitious cares and superfluously coarse labors of life that its finer fruits cannot be plucked by them. Their fingers, from excessive toil, are too clumsy and tremble too much for that. Actually, the laboring man has not leisure for a true integrity day by day; he cannot afford to sustain the manliest relations to men; his labor would be depreciated in the market. He has no time to be any thing but a machine. How can he remember well his ignorance –

which his growth requires – who has so often to use his knowledge? We should feed and clothe him gratuitously sometimes, and recruit him with our cordials, before we judge of him. The finest qualities of our nature, like the bloom on fruits, can be preserved only by the most delicate handling. Yet we do not treat ourselves nor one another thus tenderly.

Some of you, we all know, are poor, find it hard to live, are sometimes, as it were, gasping for breath. I have no doubt that some of you who read this book are unable to pay for all the dinners which you have actually eaten, or for the coats and shoes which are fast wearing or are already worn out, and have come to this page to spend borrowed or stolen time, robbing your creditors of an hour. It is very evident what mean and sneaking lives many of you live, for my sight has been whetted by experience; always on the limits, trying to get into business and trying to get out of debt, a very ancient slough, called by the Latins *æs alienum*, another's brass, for some of their coins were made of brass; still living, and dying, and buried by this other's brass; always promising to pay, promising to pay, tomorrow, and dying today, insolvent; seeking to curry favor, to get custom, by how many modes, only not state-prison offenses; lying, flattering, voting, contracting yourselves into a nutshell of civility, or dilating into an atmosphere of thin and vaporous generosity, that you may persuade your neighbor to let you make his shoes, or his hat, or his coat, or his carriage, or import his groceries for him; making yourselves sick, that you may lay up something against a sick day, something to be tucked away in an old chest, or in a stocking behind the plastering, or, more safely, in the brick bank; no matter where, no matter how much or how little.

I sometimes wonder that we can be so frivolous, I may almost say, as to attend to the gross but somewhat foreign form of servitude called Negro Slavery, there are so many keen and subtle masters that enslave both north and south. It is hard to have a southern overseer; it is worse to have a northern one; but worst of all when you are the slave-driver of yourself. Talk of a divinity in man! Look at the teamster on the highway, wending to market by day or night; does any divinity stir within him? His highest duty to fodder and water his horses! What is his destiny to him compared with the shipping interests? Does not he drive for Squire Make-a-stir? How godlike, how immortal, is he? See how he cowers and sneaks, how vaguely all the day he fears, not being immortal nor divine, but the slave and prisoner of his own opinion of himself, a fame won by his own deeds. Public opinion is a weak tyrant compared with our own private opinion. What a man thinks of himself, that it is which determines, or rather indicates, his fate. Self-emancipation even in the West Indian provinces of the fancy and imagination, — what Wilberforce is there to bring that about? Think, also, of the ladies of the land weaving toilet cushions against the last day, not to betray too green an interest in their fates! As if you could kill time without injuring eternity.

The mass of men lead lives of quiet desperation. What is called resignation is confirmed desperation. From the desperate city you go into the desperate country, and have to console yourself with the bravery of minks and muskrats. A stereotyped but unconscious despair is concealed even under what are called the games and amusements of mankind. There is no play in them, for this comes after work. But it is a characteristic of wisdom not to do desperate things.

When we consider what, to use the words of the catechism, is the chief end of man, and what are the true necessaries and means of life, it appears as if men had deliberately chosen the common mode of living because they preferred it to any other. Yet they honestly think there is no choice left. But alert and healthy natures remember that the sun rose clear. It is never too late to give up our prejudices. No way of thinking or doing, however ancient, can be trusted without proof. What every body echoes or in silence passes by as true today may turn out to be falsehood tomorrow, mere smoke of opinion, which some had trusted for a cloud that would sprinkle fertilizing rain on their fields. What old people say you cannot do you try and find that you can. Old deeds for old people, and new deeds for new. Old people did not know enough once, perchance, to fetch fresh fuel to keep the fire a-going; new people put a little dry wood under a pot, and are whirled round the globe with the speed of birds, in a way to kill old people, as the phrase is. Age is no better, hardly so well, qualified for an instructor as youth, for it has not profited so much as it has lost. One may almost doubt if the wisest man has learned any thing of absolute value by living. Practically, the old have no very important advice to give the young, their own experience has been so partial, and their lives have been such miserable failures, for private reasons, as they must believe; and it may be that they have some faith left which belies that experience, and they are only less young than they were. I have lived some thirty years on this planet, and I have yet to hear the first syllable of valuable or even earnest advice from my seniors. They have told me nothing, and probably cannot tell me any thing, to the purpose. Here is life, an experiment to a great extent untried by me;

but it does not avail me that they have tried it. If I have any experience which I think valuable, I am sure to reflect that this my Mentors said nothing about.

---

from *Poems*
WANG WEI (AD 699-761)

Wang Wei was an early Chinese loafer poet, who lived a life of inner calm.

Reply to Chang Yin

I have a cottage in the Chungnan foothills
The Chungnan mountains face it
All the year long no guests
and the gate remains shut

All the day long no plans
and I remain at leisure

Nothing to stop you taking a drink
or casting for a fish
You have only to come along
come and see me here.

Living by the River Ch'i

I am living in seclusion by the waters of the Ch'i
The land to the east is bare and without a hill
The sun is hidden beyond the mulberry trees
The river shines between the villages
Shepherd boys move off towards their far hamlets
Hunting dogs follow their masters home
And what has the man without occupation done?
He has passed the whole day behind his closed gate.

———◆———

from *Phrases and Philosophies for the Use of the Young*
OSCAR WILDE, 1894

There is something tragic about the enormous
    number
of young men there are in England at the present
    moment
who start life with perfect profiles, and end by adopting
some useful profession.

———◆———

from *Forest Notes: Idle Hours*
ROBERT LOUIS STEVENSON, 1876

Where we find Stevenson in a relaxed mood as he imagines a lone stroll through the trees.

*T*he woods by night, in all their uncanny effect, are not rightly to be understood until you can compare them with the woods by day. The stillness of the medium, the floor of glittering sand, these trees that go streaming up like monstrous sea-weeds and waver in the moving winds like the weeds in submarine currents, all these set the mind working on the thought of what you may have seen off a foreland or over the side of a boat, and make you feel like a diver, down in the quiet water, fathoms below the tumbling, transitory surface of the sea. And yet in itself, as I say, the strangeness of these nocturnal solitudes is not to be felt fully without the sense of contrast. You must have risen in the morning and seen the woods as they are by day, kindled and colored in the sun's light; you must have felt the odor of innumerable trees at even, the unsparing heat along the forest roads and the coolness of the groves.

And on the first morning, you will doubtless rise betimes. If you have not been wakened before by the visit of some adventurous pigeon, you will be wakened as soon as the sun can reach your window — for there are no blinds or shutters to keep him out — and the room, with its bare wood floor and bare whitewashed walls, shines all round you in a sort of glory of reflected lights. You may doze a while longer by snatches, or lie awake to study the charcoal-men and dogs and horses with which former occupants have defiled the partitions; Thiers, with wily profile; local celebrities, pipe in hand; or maybe a romantic landscape, splashed in oil. Meanwhile artist after artist drops into the *salle-à-manger* for coffee, and then shoulders easel, sunshade, stool, and paintbox, bound into a faggot, and sets off for what he calls his "motive." And artist after artist, as he goes out of the village, carries with him a little following of dogs. For the dogs, who belong only nominally to any special master, hang about the gate of the forest all day long, and whenever anyone goes by, who hits their fancy, profit by his escort, and go forth with him to play an hour or two at hunting. They would like to be under the trees all day. But they cannot go alone. They require a pretext. And so they take the passing artist as an excuse to go into the woods, as they might take a walking-stick as an excuse to bathe. With quick ears, long spines, and bandy legs, or perhaps as tall as a greyhound and with a bulldog's head, this company of mongrels will trot by your side all day and come home with you at night, still showing white teeth and wagging stunted tail. Their good humor is not to be exhausted. You may pelt them with stones, if you please, and all they will do is to give you a wider berth. If once they come out with you, to you they will remain faithful, and with you return; although if you meet them next morning in the street, it is as like as not they will cut you with a countenance of brass.

The forest — a strange thing for an Englishman — is very destitute of birds. This is no country where every patch of wood among the meadows gives up an incense of song, and every valley, wandered through by a streamlet, rings and reverberates from side to side with a profusion of clear notes. And this rarity of birds is not to be regretted on its own account only. For the insects prosper in their absence, and become as one of the plagues of Egypt. Ants swarm in the hot sand; mosquitoes drone their nasal drone; wherever the sun finds a hole in the roof of the forest you see a myriad transparent creatures coming and going in the shaft of light; and even between whiles, even where there is no incursion of sun-rays into the dark arcade of the wood, you are conscious of a continual drift of insects, an ebb and flow of infinitesimal living things between the trees. Nor are insects the only evil creatures that haunt the forest. For you may plump into a cave among the rocks, and find yourself face to face with a wild boar; or see a crooked viper slither across the road.

Perhaps you may set yourself down in the bay between two spreading beech-roots with a book on your lap, and be awakened all of a sudden by a friend: "I say, just keep where you are, will you? You make the jolliest motive." And you reply: "Well, I don't mind, if I may smoke." And thereafter the hours go idly by. Your friend at the easel labors doggedly, a little way off, in the wide shadow of the tree; and yet farther, across a strait of glaring sunshine, you see another painter, encamped in the shadow of another tree, and up to his waist in the fern. You cannot watch your own effigy growing out of the white trunk, and the trunk beginning to stand forth from the rest of the wood, and the whole picture getting dappled over with the flecks of sun, that slip through the leaves overhead, and as a wind goes by and sets the trees a-talking, flicker hither and thither like butterflies of light. But you know it is going forward; and, out of emulation with the painter, get ready your own palette and lay out the color for a woodland scene in words.

Your tree stands in a hollow paved with fern and heather, set in a basin of low hills, and scattered over with rocks and junipers. All the open is steeped in pitiless sunlight. Everything stands out as though it were cut in cardboard, every color is strained into its highest key. The boulders are some of them upright and dead like monolithic castles, some of them prone like sleeping cattle. The junipers — looking, in their soiled and ragged mourning, like some funeral procession that has gone seeking the place of sepulture three hundred years and more in wind and rain — are daubed in, forcibly, against the glowing ferns and heather. Every tassel of their rusty foliage is defined with pre-Raphaelite minuteness. And a sorry figure they make out there in the sun, like misbegotten yew-trees! The scene is all pitched in a key of color so peculiar, and lit up with such a discharge of violent sunlight as a man might live fifty years in England and not see.

Meanwhile at your elbow someone tunes up a song, words of Ronsard to a pathetic tremulous air, of how the poet loved his mistress long ago, and pressed on her the flight of time, and told her how white and quiet the dead lay under the stones, and how the boat dipped and pitched as the shades embarked for the passionless land. Yet a little while, sang the poet, and there shall be no more love; only to sit, and remember loves that might have been. There is a falling flourish in the air that remains in the memory and comes back in incongruous places, on the seat of hansoms or in the warm bed at night, with something of a forest savor.

"You can get up now," says the painter; "I'm at the background."

And so up you get, stretching yourself, and go your way into the wood, the daylight becoming richer and more golden, and the shadows stretching further into the open. A cool air comes along the highways, and the scents awaken. The fir-trees breathe abroad their ozone. Out of unknown thickets comes forth the soft, secret, aromatic odor of the woods, not like a smell of the free heaven, but as though court ladies, who had known these paths in ages long gone by, still walked in the summer evenings, and shed, from their brocades, a breath of musk or bergamot upon the woodland winds. One side of the long avenues is still kindled with the sun, the other is plunged in transparent shadow. Over the trees, the west begins to burn like a furnace; and the painters gather up their chattels, and go down, by avenue or footpath, to the plain.

from *Damien Hirst Interview*
THE IDLER, NO. 10, 1995

IDLER: What's idleness for you?

HIRST: It's about minimum effort, maximum effect. And it's about people who work and play in a way in which you can't separate one from the other. It's like when a car is idling. You have the possibility of going somewhere, but you're not going anywhere. But that doesn't mean you're not doing anything. The energy's there. I could very easily make shitloads of money, I know exactly how to do it. But I know if I did it, it's a slow decline into nothing. Whereas if I constantly make an effort to be more than that, to compromise without compromise . . . that means you really give someone what they want to get what you want. So in a way it's a compromise, but you get so much of what you want that you're not really compromising.

---

from *Lost Horizon*
JAMES HILTON, 1933

In Lost Horizon, *a group of Westerners find themselves captured by Lamas in the mountains of Tibet. Here the drifter of the group, Conway, swaps thoughts with a Tibetan holy man.*

"Slackers?" queried Chang. His knowledge of English was extremely good, but sometimes a colloquialism proved unfamiliar.

"Slacker," explained Conway, "is a slang word meaning a lazy fellow, a good-for-nothing. I wasn't, of course, using it seriously."

Chang bowed his thanks for the information. He took a

keen interest in languages, and liked to weigh a new word philosophically. "It is significant," he said after a pause, "that the English regard slackness as a vice. We, on the other hand, should vastly prefer it to tension. Is there not too much tension in the world at present, and might it not be better if more people were slackers?"

"I'm inclined to agree with you," Conway answered with solemn amusement.

the Unemployed

For those of us who get paid by the hour, it is hard not to feel bitter that – if we end up old and rich – we will not be able to pay to get those hours back. The time into money exchange goes only one way, and in a direction that is rarely to our advantage.

The problem of balancing time and money, the cult of work and the office, are ideas that are becoming increasingly open to question. In this section we present writers who have both questioned the very core of the work ethic and attempted to reach an amicable compromise between the demands of an employer, and the right to live a decent life.

Some of the following extracts brush against the political dimension of idleness, what it means as a gesture to remove oneself from wages and the accumulation of possessions. Of course if idlers are to head a revolution against job insecurity, meager pay, unreasonable hours, job dissatisfaction, it will be – in the words of D.H. Lawrence – a revolution for fun. Roll on the day when we can replace the knuckle-tattoos of "love" and "hate" with "work" and "play."

Wages
from *Pansies, 1928–29*

D.H. LAWRENCE

The wages of work is cash.
The wages of cash is want more cash.
The wages of want more cash is vicious competition.
The wages of vicious competition is — the world we live
    in.

The work-cash-want circle is the viciousest circle
that ever turned men into fiends.

Earning a wage is a prison occupation
and a wage-earner is a sort of gaol-bird.

Earning a salary is a prison overseer's job
a gaoler instead of a gaol-bird.

Living on our income is strolling grandly outside the
    prison
in terror lest you have to go in. And since the work-
    prison covers
almost every scrap of the living earth, you stroll up and
    down
on a narrow beat, about the same as a prisoner taking
    his exercise.

This is called universal freedom.

from *Utopia*

SIR THOMAS MORE, 1516

By a curious historical twist, it appears that Thomas More's vision of utopia is ripe for reinterpretation as a hot new management theory book.

You see how it is — wherever you are, you always have to work. There's never any excuse for idleness. There are also no wine-taverns, no ale-houses, no brothels, no opportunities for seduction, no secret meeting-places. Everyone has his eye on you, so you're practically forced to get on with your job, and make some proper use of your spare time.

---

from *The Right to be Lazy*

PAUL LAFARGUE, 1883

Paul Lafargue's radical satire on the cult of labor and the working classes aroused one or two murmurs of discontent from his industrious father-in-law, Karl Marx.

> Let us be lazy in everything,
> except in loving and drinking,
> except in being lazy.
>
> LESSING

I. A Disastrous Dogma

A strange delusion possesses the working classes of the nations where capitalist civilization holds its sway. This delusion drags in its train the individual and social woes which for two centuries have tortured sad humanity. This delusion is the love of work, the furious passion for work, pushed even to the exhaustion of the vital force of the individual and his progeny. Instead of opposing this mental aberration, the priests, the economists and the moralists have cast a sacred halo over work. Blind and finite men, they have wished to be wiser than their God; weak and contemptible men, they have presumed to rehabilitate what their God had cursed. I, who do not profess to be a Christian, an economist or a moralist, I appeal from their judgment to that of their God; from the preachings of their religious, economic or free-thought ethics, to the frightful consequences of work in capitalist society.

In capitalist society work is the cause of all intellectual degeneracy, of all organic deformity. Compare the thorough-bred in Rothschild's stables, served by a retinue of bipeds, with the heavy brute of the Norman farms which

[1] European explorers pause in wonder before the physical beauty and the proud bearing of the men of primitive races, not soiled by what Paeppig calls "the poisonous breath of civilization." Speaking of the aborigines of the Oceanic Islands, Lord George Campbell writes: "There is not a people in the world which strikes one more favorably at first sight. Their smooth skin of a light copper tint, their hair golden and curly, their beautiful and happy faces, in a word, their whole person formed a new and splendid specimen of the 'genus homo,' their physical appearance gave the impression of a race superior to ours." The civilized men of ancient Rome, witness Caesar and Tacitus, regarded with the same admiration the Germans of the communist tribes which invaded the Roman empire. Following Tacitus, Salvien, the priest of the fifth century who received the surname of master of the Bishops, held up the barbarians as an example to civilized Christians: "We are immodest before the barbarians, who are more chaste than we. Even more the barbarians are wounded at our lack of modesty; the Goths do not permit debauchees of their own nation to remain among them; alone

plows the earth, carts the manure, hauls the crops. Look at
the noble savage whom the missionaries of trade and the
traders of religion have not yet corrupted with Christianity, syphilis and the dogma of work, and then look at our
miserable slaves of machines.[1]

When, in our civilized Europe, we would find a trace of
the native beauty of man, we must go seek it in the nations
where economic prejudices have not yet uprooted the hatred of work. Spain, which, alas, is degenerating, may still
boast of possessing fewer factories than we have of prisons
and barracks; but the artist rejoices in his admiration of the

in the midst of them, by the sad privilege of their nationality and
their name, the Romans have the right to be impure. (Pederasty
was then the height of the fashion among both pagans and Christians.) The oppressed fly to the barbarians to seek for mercy and a
shelter." (De Gubernatione Dei.) The old civilization and the rising
Christianity corrupted the barbarians of the ancient world, as the
old Christianity and the modern capitalist civilization are corrupt-
ing the savages of the new world.

M. F. LePlay, whose talent for observation must be recognized,
even if we reject his sociological conclusions, tainted with philan-
thropic and Christian pharisaism, says in his book "Les Ouvriers
Européens" (1885): "The Propensity of the Bachkirs for laziness (the
Bachkirs are semi-nomadic shepherds of the Asiatic slope of the
Ural mountains); the leisure of nomadic life, the habit of medita-
tion which this engenders in the best endowed individuals,—all
this often gives them a distinction of manner, a fineness of intelligence and judgment which is rarely to be observed on the same
social level in a more developed civilization . . . The thing most
repugnant to them is agricultural labor: they will do anything
rather than accept the trade of farmer." Agriculture is in fact the
first example of servile labor in the history of man. According to
biblical tradition, the first criminal, Cain, is a farmer.

hardy Andalusian, brown as his native chestnuts, straight and flexible as a steel rod; and the heart leaps at hearing the beggar, superbly draped in his ragged *capa*, parleying on terms of equality with the duke of Ossuna. For the Spaniard, in whom the primitive animal has not been atrophied, work is the worst sort of slavery.[2] The Greeks in their era of greatness had only contempt for work: their slaves alone were permitted to labor: the free man knew only exercises for the body and mind. And so it was in this era that men like Aristotle, Phidias, Aristophanes moved and breathed among the people; it was the time when a handful of heroes at Marathon crushed the hordes of Asia, soon to be subdued by Alexander. The philosophers of antiquity taught contempt for work, that degradation of the free man, the poets sang of idleness, that gift from the Gods:

> *O Melibae Deus nobis haec otia fecit.*[3]

Jesus, in his sermon on the Mount, preached idleness: "Consider the lilies of the field, how they grow: they toil not, neither do they spin: and yet I say unto you that even Solomon in all his glory was not arrayed like one of these." Jehovah the bearded and angry god, gave his worshipers the supreme example of ideal laziness; after six days of work, he rests for all eternity.

On the other hand, what are the races for which work is an organic necessity? The Auvergnians; the Scotch, those Auvergnians of the British Isles; the Galicians, those Auvergnians of Spain; the Pomeranians, those Auvergnians of

---

[2] The Spanish proverb says: Descanzar es salud. (Rest is healthful.)
[3] O Melibaeus! a god has granted us this idleness. Virgil, *Bucolics*

Germany; the Chinese, those Auvergnians of Asia. In our society, which are the classes that love work for work's sake? The peasant proprietors, the little shopkeepers; the former bent double over their fields, the latter crouched in their shops, burrow like the mole in his subterranean passage and never stand up to look at nature leisurely.

And meanwhile the proletariat, the great class embracing all the producers of civilized nations, the class which in freeing itself will free humanity from servile toil and will make of the human animal a free being, – the proletariat, betraying its instincts, despising its historic mission, has let itself be perverted by the dogma of work. Rude and terrible has been its punishment. All its individual and social woes are born of its passion for work.

---

from *Who Will Do the Dirty Work?*
TONY GIBSON, 1952

This tract was conceived to answer that pressing sociological question: in an anarchist society, who will clean the sewers?

Do we have to look further for the roots of all social disharmony and individual misery of our time? With us, work is generally regarded as a regrettable necessity, an activity to be endured only for the sake of the material goods produced, or rather for the wage packet which bears no obvious relationship to the work done. The best that reformers, social planners and even social revolutionaries can suggest is that we may make the working day shorter, so that there will be less pain (work) and more pleasure (idleness) in our lives. I have even heard an anarchist meeting discussing whether in the great and glorious by-and-by we should have to do three hours work a day or three hours work a week. This is strictly comparable to the following extract from an American sex-instruction manual:

> "*Question:* How long does the penis have to stay in the vagina?
> *Answer:* Only a few minutes."

Another regrettable necessity!

I do not care if in a social state of anarchy we work a great deal longer than we do today under capitalism. What I am concerned about is that the work itself shall be intrinsically satisfying. I see no other way of ensuring this than the abandonment of coercion as the mainspring of production.

---

from *The Right to Useful Unemployment*
IVAN ILLICH, 1978

One of the foremost critics of "professions," Illich points out how the modern labor market removes any opportunity for the unemployed to use their skills in the community.

At present, every new need that is professionally certified translates sooner or later into a right. The political pressure for the enactment of each right generates new jobs and commodities. Each new commodity degrades an activity by which people so far have been able to cope on their own; each new job takes away legitimacy from work so far done by the unemployed. The power of professions to measure what shall be good, right, and done warps the desire, willingness, and ability of the "common" man to live within his measure.

As soon as all law students currently registered at United States law schools are graduated, the number of United States lawyers will increase by about 50 per cent. Judicare will complement Medicare, as legal insurance increasingly turns into the kind of necessity that medical insurance is now. When the right of the citizen to a lawyer has been established, settling the dispute in the pub will be branded unenlightened or anti-social, as home births are now. Already the right of each citizen of Detroit to live in a home that has been professionally wired turns the auto-electrician who installs his own plugs into a lawbreaker. The loss of one liberty after another to be useful when out of a job or outside professional control is the unnamed, but also the most resented experience that comes with modernized poverty. By now the most significant privilege of high social status might well be some vestige of freedom for useful unemployment that is increasingly denied to the great majority. The insistence on the right to be taken care of and supplied has almost turned into the right of industries and professions to conquer clients, to supply them with their product, and by their deliveries to obliterate the environmental conditions that make unemployed activities useful. Thus, for the time being, the struggle for an equitable distribution of the time and the power to be useful to self and others outside employment or the draft has been effectively paralyzed. Work done off the paid job is looked down upon if not ignored. Autonomous activity threatens the employment level, generates deviance, and detracts from the GNP: therefore it is only improperly called "work." Labor no longer means effort or toil but the mysterious mate wedded to productive investments in plant. Work no longer means the creation of a value per-

ceived by the worker but mainly a job, which is a social relationship. Unemployment means sad idleness, rather
than the freedom to do things that are useful for oneself or
for one's neighbor. An active woman who runs a house
and brings up children and takes in those of others is distinguished from a woman who "works," no matter how
useless or damaging the product of this work might be.
Activity, effort, achievement, or service outside a hierar-
chical relationship and unmeasured by professional standards, threatens a commodity-intensive society. The
generation of use-values that escape effective measurement limits not only the need for more commodities but
also the jobs that create them and the paychecks needed to
buy them.

What counts in a market-intensive society is not the
effort to please or the pleasure that flows from that effort
but the coupling of the labor force with capital. What
counts is not the achievement of satisfaction that flows
from action but the status of the social relationship that
commands production — that is, the job, situation, post, or
appointment. In the Middle Ages there was no salvation
outside the Church, and the theologians had a hard time
explaining what God did with those pagans who were visibly virtuous or saintly. Similarly, in contemporary society
effort is not productive unless it is done at the behest of a
boss, and economists have a hard time dealing with the obvious usefulness of people when they are outside the corporate control of a corporation, volunteer agency, or labor
camp. Work is productive, respectable, worthy of the citizen only when the work process is planned, monitored,
and controlled by a professional agent, who ensures that
the work meets a certified need in a standardized fashion. In

an advanced industrial society it becomes almost impossible to seek, even to imagine, unemployment as a condition for autonomous, useful work. The infrastructure of society is so arranged that only the job gives access to the tools of production, and this monopoly of commodity production over the generation of use-values turns even more stringent as the state takes over. Only with a license may you teach a child; only at a clinic may you set a broken bone. Housework, handicrafts, subsistence agriculture, radical technology, learning exchanges, and the like are degraded into activities for the idle, the unproductive, the very poor, or the very rich. A society that fosters intense dependence on commodities thus turns its unemployed into either its poor or its dependents. In 1945, for each American Social Security recipient there were still 35 workers on the job. In 1977, 3.2 employed workers have to support one such retiree, who is himself dependent on many more services than his retired grandfather could have imagined.

Henceforth the quality of a society and of its culture will depend on the status of its unemployed: will they be the most representative productive citizens, or will they be dependents? The choice or crisis again seems clear: advanced industrial society can degenerate into a holding operation harking back to the dream of the sixties; into a well-rationed distribution system that doles out decreasing commodities and jobs and trains its citizens for more standardized consumption and more powerless work. This is the attitude reflected in the policy proposals of most governments at present, from Germany to China, albeit a fundamental difference in degree: the richer the country, the more urgent it seems to ration access to jobs and to impede useful unemployment that would threaten the volume of the labor market. The inverse, of course, is equally possible: a modern society in which frustrated workers organize to protect the freedom of people to be useful outside the activities that result in the production of commodities. But again, this social alternative depends on a new, rational, and cynical competence of the common man when faced with the professional imputation of needs.

———

from *Interview with Charles Handy*
THE IDLER, NO. 3, 1994

Author of The Empty Raincoat, *Charles Handy is one of the best-selling management theorists.*

IDLER: People's identities tend to be bound up with their job. At parties, people ask each other "what do you do?" You can sense the tension at parties of people in their early twenties. If you don't have a conventional career or a job it's a difficult question to answer.

HANDY: You can play the trick the other way round. There was a time when I got so fed up with people asking me what I did — because it wasn't very exciting, I was just an oil executive — that I took to saying "nothing." And you should watch the look on people's faces when you say "nothing," because they don't know whether to be embarrassed because "oh gosh you're unemployed," or whether you're very rich and don't need to work. They just didn't know how to respond, it was marvelous. It's quite interesting that in Italy you tend to say "where do you live," rather than "what do you do."

IDLER: The Italians seem to be good at positive idleness.

HANDY: The Italians do work hard but they don't think that work is the most important thing in life. The important thing in life is in a sense living, and that means eating, drinking and having *la bella figura* – putting on a good appearance in the street. A lot of the life is lived in the street. They told me how odd it is in England when you go to any kind of party or meal everybody talks not about the weather but about the traffic – how did you get here, what was it like. In Italy, they said, we wouldn't dream of talking about the traffic, which is terrible, we always talk about food. That fits another part of my philosophy which I call the doughnut philosophy of life. I believe you should look at life as an inside-out doughnut, where the hole is on the outside and the dough is in the middle. There should be a core to your life, to do with earning money, having a house or whatever, but if you let that core fill the whole of the doughnut, you are missing out on a lot. Somebody once said that by the time you die you've only discovered 25% of what you're capable of. It's unprovable but possibly true, and the reason is that people don't experiment enough with life; they let work fill up the doughnut. There's an awful lot of interesting space there, but you have to organize yourself to do it.

IDLER: That's the key thing, what we call the struggle to idleness – trying to gain control of your own life, to allow yourself three months in Tuscany or whatever it is.

HANDY: It's very important you do. People let other people control their lives. You can also look at it in a quite different way. Ten years ago, when I became totally freelance, my wife Liz and I worked out that out of the 365 days of the year we needed 100 days to make serious money – I do that by teaching at various seminars. I also need 100 days a year to write and read, and roughly 50 days a year for my causes and campaigns. That leaves 115 days which we can use for our own pursuits. That's actually very mean to ourselves in a way, because most people have at least that if you add up all the weekends, eight public holidays plus whatever holidays they're entitled to. But by chunking it that way we can spend 90 days sitting doing nothing – except eating, drinking and discovering Italy in Tuscany.

IDLER: You were saying that it amazes you how few people are trying to take control of their lives.

HANDY: For some reason, most people still want to sell their time to an organization. I did that once, when I was helping to start the London Business School. I worked terribly hard; I used to leave home at half past seven and I'd come home at nine. My wife said to me after about three years of this: "I know you're pleased with what you're doing, I just have to tell you you've become the most boring man I've ever met."

IDLER: One thing that's been worrying me recently is how every office, without exception, seems to be packed to the brim with hideous office politics. I wonder how much this has got to do with the people and how much with the actual structure of the place, the office itself.

HANDY: If you put a lot of rats in a small space, they fight. It's true. If you put a lot of pigs in a small place they scratch each other's tails off. If you put them in a great big field with lots of space around them they're fine, they're relaxed. Shoving everybody together is crazy. I walk through the City and I look up at these little boxes piled sky-high – we actually seem to want to go and spend our days sitting in a little box. It's terrifying. Luckily I think that's going to break down. It's very expensive to organizations to bring people in from their homes in the countryside and put them in these boxes. Interestingly they are there for 168 hours a week, but are only used for maybe 50 or 60 hours a week. It's an extraordinarily bad use of space. It would be much better to let them pay for their space, by working from home, in the car, on the train or in the client's premises, and connecting up with telephones. If you do that then you have more control over your time. Also, it's terribly difficult for women now who want to have a career but also want to raise a family. But it need not be difficult because they can perfectly well do an awful lot of their work without going into the office. They can go into the office two or three times a week. Organizations should say, "all our meetings are going to take place on Tuesday, Wednesday, Thursday mornings, and everything else is your time, to be used at your discretion." We're not running factories any more. You don't have to be together all the time, just for bits of time. And so in fact we don't need all these offices. We say we want them for companionship, but you're absolutely right, companionship turns into office politics.

In Praise of Idleness
BERTRAND RUSSELL, 1932

This essay is one of the core texts in The Idler *canon and appears here in edited form. It draws a vital distinction between those who loaf and those who loaf on the back of the labor of others.*

A great deal of harm is being done in the modern world by belief in the virtuousness of WORK, and that the road to happiness and prosperity lies in an organized diminution of work.

First of all: what is work? Work is of two kinds: first, altering the position of matter at or near the earth's surface relatively to other such matter; second, telling other people to do so. The first kind is unpleasant and ill paid, the second is pleasant and highly paid. The second kind is capable of indefinite extension: there are not only those who give orders, but those who give advice as to what orders should be given. Usually two opposite kinds of advice are given simultaneously by two organized bodies of men; this is called politics. The skill required for this kind of work is not knowledge of the subjects as to which advice is given, but knowledge of the art of persuasive speaking and writing, i.e. of advertising.

Throughout Europe, though not in America, there is a third class of men, more respected than either of the classes of workers. There are men who, through ownership of land, are able to make others pay for the privilege of being allowed to exist and to work. These landowners are idle, and I might therefore be expected to praise them. Unfortunately, their idleness is only rendered possible by the industry of others; indeed their desire for comfortable idleness is historically the source of the whole gospel of work. The last thing they have ever wished is that others should follow their example.

From the beginning of civilization until the Industrial Revolution, a man could, as a rule, produce by hard work little more than was required for the subsistence of himself and his family, although his wife worked at least as hard as he did, and his children added their labor as soon as they were old enough to do so. The small surplus above bare necessaries was not left to those who produced it, but was appropriated by warriors and priests. In times of famine there was no surplus; the warriors and priests, however, still secured as much as at other times, with the result that many of the workers died of hunger. This system persisted in Russia until 1917, and still persists in the East; in England, in spite of the Industrial Revolution, it remained in full force throughout the Napoleonic wars, and until a hundred years ago, when the new class of manufacturers acquired power. In America, the system came to an end with the Revolution, except in the South, where it persisted until the Civil War. A system which lasted so long and ended so recently has naturally left a profound impress upon men's thoughts and opinions. Much that we take for granted about the desirability of work is derived from this system, and, being pre-industrial, is not adapted to the modern world. Modern technique has made it possible for leisure, within limits, to be not the prerogative of small privileged classes, but a right evenly distributed throughout the community. The morality of work is the morality of slaves, and the modern world has no need of slavery.

It is obvious that, in primitive communities, peasants, left to themselves, would not have parted with the slender surplus upon which the warriors and priests subsisted, but would have either produced less or consumed more. At first, sheer force compelled them to produce and part with the surplus. Gradually, however, it was found possible to induce many of them to accept an ethic according to which it was their duty to work hard, although part of their work went to support others in idleness. By this means the amount of compulsion required was lessened, and the expenses of government were diminished. To this day, 99 per cent of British wage-earners would be genuinely shocked if it were proposed that the King should not have larger income than a working man. The conception of duty, speaking historically, has been a means used by the holders of power to induce others to live for the interests of their masters rather than for their own. Of course the holders of power conceal this fact from themselves by managing to believe that their interests are identical with the larger interests of humanity. Sometimes this is true; Athenian slave-owners, for instance, employed part of their leisure in making a permanent contribution to civilization which would have been impossible under a just economic system. Leisure is essential to civilization, and in former times leisure for the few was only rendered possible by the labors of the many. But their labors were valuable, not because work is good, but because leisure is good. And with modern technique it would be possible to distribute leisure justly without injury to civilization.

Modern technique has made it possible to diminish enormously the amount of labor required to secure the necessaries of life for everyone. This was made obvious during the war. At that time, all the men in the armed forces, all the men and women engaged in the production of munitions, all the men and women engaged in spying, war propaganda, or Government offices connected with the war, were withdrawn from productive occupation. In spite of this, the general level of physical well-being among unskilled wage-earners on the side of the Allies was higher than before or since. The significance of this fact was concealed by finance: borrowing made it appear as if the future was nourishing the present. But that, of course, would have been impossible; a man cannot eat a loaf of bread that does not yet exist. The war showed conclusively that, by the scientific organization of production, it is possible to keep modern populations in fair comfort on a small part of the working capacity of the modern world. If, at the end of the war, the scientific organization, which had been created in order to liberate men for fighting and munition work, had been preserved, and the hours of work had been cut down to four, all would have been well. Instead of that the old chaos was restored, those whose work was demanded were made to work long hours, and the rest were left to starve as unemployed. Why? because work is a duty, and a man should not receive wages in proportion to what he has produced, but in proportion to his virtue as exemplified by his industry.

This is the morality of the Slave State, applied in circumstances totally unlike those in which it arose. No wonder the result has been disastrous. Let us take an illustration. Suppose that, at a given moment, a certain number of people are engaged in the manufacture of pins. They make as many pins as the world needs, working (say) eight hours a day. Someone makes an invention by which the same number of men can make twice as many pins as before. But the world does not need twice as many pins: pins are already so cheap that hardly any more will be bought at a lower price. In a sensible world, everybody concerned in the manufacture of pins would take to working four hours instead of eight, and everything else would go on as before. But in the actual world this would be thought demoralizing. The men still work eight hours, there are too many pins, some employers go bankrupt, and half the men previously concerned in making pins are thrown out of work. There is, in the end, just as much leisure as on the other plan, but half the men are totally idle while half are still overworked. In this way, it is ensured that the unavoidable leisure shall cause misery all round instead of being a universal source of happiness. Can anything more insane be imagined?

The idea that the poor should have leisure has always been shocking to the rich. In England, in the early nineteenth century, fifteen hours was the ordinary day's work for a man; children sometimes did as much, and very commonly did twelve hours a day. When meddlesome busybodies suggested that perhaps these hours were rather long, they were told that work kept adults from drink and children from mischief. When I was a child, shortly after urban working men had acquired the vote, certain public holidays were established by law, to the great indignation of the upper classes. I remember hearing an old Duchess say: "What do the poor want with holidays? They ought to *work*." People nowadays are less frank, but the sentiment persists, and is the source of much of our economic confusion.

Let us, for a moment, consider the ethics of work frankly, without superstition. Every human being, of necessity, consumes, in the course of his life, a certain amount of the produce of human labor. Assuming, as we may, that labor is on the whole disagreeable, it is unjust that a man should consume more than he produces. Of course he may provide services rather than commodities, like a medical man, for example; but he should provide something in return for his board and lodging. To this extent, the duty of work must be admitted, but to this extent only.

I shall not dwell upon the fact that, in all modern societies outside the U.S.S.R., many people escape even this minimum of work, namely all those who inherit money and all those who marry money. I do not think the fact that these people are allowed to be idle is nearly so harmful as the fact that wage-earners are expected to overwork or starve.

If the ordinary wage-earner worked four hours a day, there would be enough for everybody, and no unemployment — assuming a certain very moderate amount of sensible organization. This idea shocks the well-to-do, because they are convinced that the poor would not know how to use so much leisure. In America, men often work long hours even when they are already well off; such men, naturally, are indignant at the idea of leisure for wage-earners, except as the grim punishment of unemployment; in fact, they dislike leisure even for their sons. Oddly enough, while they wish their sons to work so hard as to have no time to be civilized, they do not mind their wives and daughters having no work at all. The snobbish admiration of uselessness, which, in an aristocratic society, extends to both sexes, is, under a plutocracy, confined to women; this, however, does not make it any more in agreement with common sense.

The wise use of leisure, it must be conceded, is a product of civilization and education. A man who has worked long hours all his life will be bored if he becomes suddenly idle. But without a considerable amount of leisure a man is cut off from many of the best things. There is no longer any reason why the bulk of the population should suffer this deprivation; only a foolish asceticism, usually vicarious, makes us continue to insist on work in excessive quantities now that the need no longer exists.

In the new creed which controls the government of Russia, while there is much that is very different from the traditional teaching of the West, there are some things that are quite unchanged. The attitude of the governing classes, and especially of those who conduct educational propaganda, on the subject of the dignity of labor, is almost exactly that which the governing classes of the world have always preached to what were called the "honest poor." Industry, sobriety, willingness to work long hours for distant advantages, even submissiveness to authority, all these reappear; moreover authority still represents the will of the Ruler of the Universe, Who, however, is now called by a new name, Dialectical Materialism.

The victory of the proletariat in Russia has some points in common with the victory of the feminists in some other countries. For ages, men had conceded the superior saintliness of women, and had consoled women for their inferiority by maintaining that saintliness is more desirable than power. At last the feminists decided that they would have both, since the pioneers among them believed all that the men had told them about the desirability of virtue, but not what they had told them about the worthlessness of political power. A similar thing has happened in Russia as regards manual work. For ages, the rich and their sycophants have written in praise of "honest toil," have praised the simple life, have professed a religion which teaches that the poor are much more likely to go to heaven than the rich, and in general have tried to make manual workers believe that there is some special nobility about altering the position of matter in space, just as men tried to make women believe that they derived some special nobility from their sexual enslavement. In Russia, all this teaching about the excellence of manual work has been taken seriously, with the result that the manual worker is more honored than anyone else. What are, in essence, revivalist appeals are made, but not for the old purposes: they are made to secure shock workers for special tasks. Manual work is the ideal which is held before the young, and is the basis of all ethical teaching.

For the present, possibly, this is all to the good. A large country, full of natural resources, awaits development, and has to be developed with very little use of credit. In these circumstances, hard work is necessary, and is likely to bring a great reward. But what will happen when the point has been reached where everybody could be comfortable without working long hours?

In the West, we have various ways of dealing with this problem. We have no attempt at economic justice, so that a large proportion of the total produce goes to a small minority of the population, many of whom do no work at all. Owing to the absence of any central control over production, we produce hosts of things that are not wanted. We keep a large percentage of the working population idle, because we can dispense with their labor by making the others overwork. When all these methods prove inadequate, we have a war: we cause a number of people to manufacture high explosives, and a number of others to explode them, as if we were children who had just discovered fireworks. By a combination of all these devices we manage, though with difficulty, to keep alive the notion that a great deal of severe manual work must be the lot of the average man.

In Russia, owing to more economic justice and central control over production, the problem will have to be differently solved. The rational solution would be, as soon as the necessaries and elementary comforts can be provided for all, to reduce the hours of labor gradually, allow-ing a popular vote to decide, at each stage, whether more leisure or more goods were to be preferred. But, having taught the supreme virtue of hard work, it is difficult to see how the authorities can aim at a paradise in which there will be much leisure and little work. It seems more likely that they will find continually fresh schemes, by which present leisure is to be sacrificed to future productivity. I read recently of an ingenious plan put forward by Russian engineers, for making the White Sea and the northern coasts of Siberia warm, by putting a dam across the Kara Sea. An admirable project, but liable to postpone proletar-ian comfort for a generation, while the nobility of toil is be-ing displayed amid the icefields and snowstorms of the Arctic Ocean. This sort of thing, if it happens, will be the result of regarding the virtue of hard work as an end in it-self, rather than as a means to a state of affairs in which it is no longer needed.

The fact is that moving matter about, while a certain amount of it is necessary to our existence, is emphatically not one of the ends of human life. If it were, we should have to consider every navvy superior to Shakespeare. We have been misled in this matter by two causes. One is the necessity of keeping the poor contented, which has led the rich, for thousands of years, to preach the dignity of labor, while taking care themselves to remain undignified in this respect. The other is the new pleasure in mechanism, which makes us delight in the astonishingly clever changes that we can produce on the earth's surface. Nei-ther of these motives makes any great appeal to the actual worker. If you ask him what he thinks the best part of his life, he is not likely to say: I enjoy manual work because it makes me feel that I am fulfilling man's noblest task, and because I like to think how much man can transform his planet. It is true that my body demands periods of rest, which I have to fill in as best I may, but I am never so happy as when the morning comes and I can return to the toil from which my contentment springs. I have never heard working men say this sort of thing. They consider work, as it should be considered, a necessary means to a livelihood, and it is from their leisure hours that they derive whatever happiness they may enjoy.

It will be said that, while a little leisure is pleasant, men would not know how to fill their days if they had only four hours of work out of the twenty-four. In so far as this is true in the modern world, it is a condemnation of our civilization; it would not have been true at any earlier period. There was formerly a capacity for light-heartedness and play which has been to some extent inhibited by the cult of efficiency. The modern man thinks that everything ought to be done for the sake of something else, and never for its own sake. Serious-minded persons, for example, are continually condemning the habit of going to the cinema, and telling us that it leads the young into crime. But all the work that goes to producing a cinema is respectable, because it is work, and because it brings a money profit. The notion that the desirable activities are those that bring a profit has made everything topsy-turvy. The butcher who provides you with meat and the baker who provides you with bread are praiseworthy, because they are making money; but when you enjoy the food they have provided, you are merely frivolous, unless you eat only to get strength for your work. Broadly speaking, it is held that getting money is good and spending money is bad. Seeing that they are two sides of one transaction, this is absurd; one might as well maintain that keys are good, but key-holes are bad. Whatever merit there may be in the production of goods must be entirely derivative from the advantage to be obtained by consuming them. The individual, in our society, works for profit; but the social purpose of his work lies in the consumption of what he produces. It is this divorce between the individual and the social purpose of production that makes it so difficult for men to think clearly in a world in which profit-making is the incentive to industry. We think too much of production, and too little of consumption. One result is that we attach too little importance to enjoyment and simple happiness, and that we do not judge production by the pleasure that it gives to the consumer.

When I suggest that working hours should be reduced to four, I am not meaning to imply that all the remaining time should necessarily be spent in pure frivolity. I mean that four hours' work a day should entitle a man to the necessities and elementary comforts of life, and that the rest of his time should be his to use as he might see fit. It is an essential part of any such social system that education should be carried further than it usually is at present, and should aim, in part, at providing tastes which would enable a man to use leisure intelligently. I am not thinking mainly of the sort of things that would be considered "highbrow." Peasant dances have died out except in remote rural areas, but the impulses which caused them to be cultivated must still exist in human nature. The pleasures of urban populations have become mainly passive: seeing cinemas, watching football matches, listening to the radio, and so on. This results from the fact that their active energies are fully taken up with work; if they had more leisure, they would again enjoy pleasures in which they took an active part.

In the past, there was a small leisure class and a larger working class. The leisure class enjoyed advantages for which there was no basis in social justice; this necessarily made it oppressive, limited its sympathies, and caused it to invent theories by which to justify its privileges. These facts greatly diminished its excellence, but in spite of this drawback it contributed nearly the whole of what we call civilization. It cultivated the arts and discovered the sciences; it wrote the books, invented the philosophies, and refined social relations. Even the liberation of the oppressed has usually been inaugurated from above. Without the leisure class, mankind would never have emerged from barbarism.

The method of a hereditary leisure class without duties was, however, extraordinarily wasteful. None of the members of the class had been taught to be industrious, and the class as a whole was not exceptionally intelligent. The class might produce one Darwin, but against him had to be set tens of thousands of country gentlemen who never thought of anything more intelligent than fox-hunting and punishing poachers. At present, the universities are supposed to provide, in a more systematic way, what the leisure class provided accidentally and as a by-product. This is a great improvement, but it has certain drawbacks. University life is so different from life in the world at large that men who live in an academic *milieu* tend to be unaware of the preoccupations and problems of ordinary men and women; moreover their ways of expressing themselves are usually such as to rob their opinions of the influence that they ought to have upon the general public. Another disadvantage is that in universities studies are organized, and the man who thinks of some original line of research is likely to be discouraged. Academic institutions, therefore, useful as they are, are not adequate guardians of the interests of civilization in a world where everyone outside their walls is too busy for unutilitarian pursuits.

In a world where no one is compelled to work more than four hours a day, every person possessed of scientific curiosity will be able to indulge it, and every painter will be able to paint without starving, however excellent his pictures may be. Young writers will not be obliged to draw attention to themselves by sensational pot-boilers, with a view to acquiring the economic independence needed for monumental works, for which, when the time at last comes, they will have lost the taste and the capacity. Men who, in their professional work, have become interested in some phase of economics of government, will be able to develop their ideas without the academic detachment that makes the work of university economists often seem lacking in reality. Medical men will have time to learn about the progress of medicine, teachers will not be exasperatedly struggling to teach by routine methods things which they learned in their youth, which may, in the interval have been proved to be untrue.

Above all, there will be happiness and joy of life, instead of frayed nerves, weariness, and dyspepsia. The work exacted will be enough to make leisure delightful, but not enough to produce exhaustion. Since men will not be tired in their spare time, they will not demand only such amusements as are passive and vapid. At least one percent will probably devote the time not spent in professional work to pursuits of some public importance, and, since they will not depend upon these pursuits for their livelihood, their originality will be unhampered, and there will be no need to conform to the standards set by elderly pundits. But it is not only in these exceptional cases that the advantages of leisure will appear. Ordinary men and women, having the opportunity of a happy life, will become more kindly and less persecuting and less inclined to view others with suspicion. The taste for war will die out, partly for this reason, and partly because it will involve long and severe work for all. Good nature is, of all moral qualities, the one that the world needs most, and good nature is the result of ease and security, not of a life of arduous struggle. Modern methods of production have given us the possibility of ease and security for all; we have chosen, instead, to have overwork for some and starvation for others. Hitherto we have continued to be as energetic as we were before there were machines; in this we have been foolish, but there is no reason to go on being foolish for ever.

---

from *Interview with Terence McKenna*

THE IDLER, NO. I, 1993

An expert in mycology and foremost spokesman for psychoactive drugs (particularly DMT, the food of the gods) McKenna achieved notoriety when he suggested that the origin of consciousness, the catalyst in man's evolution, was in fact the magic mushroom.

IDLER: Russell wrote an essay called "In Praise of Idleness," where he argued that a new machine in a factory should lead not to the redundancy of half the workers, but to a reduction by half of the working day. I wonder why we haven't managed to organize society along those lines?

MCKENNA: I think the reason we don't organize society in that way can be summed up in the aphorism, *idle hands are the devil's tool*. In other words, institutions fear idle populations because an Idler is a thinker and thinkers are not a welcome addition to most social situations. Thinkers become malcontents, that's almost a substitute word for idle, "malcontent." Essentially, we are all kept very busy, and if you do have a moment of leisure time, then you're expected to imbibe the sanitized data stream that the cultural imprimatur has been placed upon [I believe here that McKenna is referring to watching TV]. Under no circumstances are you to actually quietly inspect the contents of your own mind. Freud called introspection "morbid" — unhealthy, introverted, antisocial, possibly neurotic, potentially pathological.

---

from *The Soul of Man Under Socialism*
OSCAR WILDE, 1891

Up to the present, man has been, to a certain extent, the slave of machinery, and there is something tragic in the fact that as soon as man had invented a machine to do his work he began to starve. This, however, is, of course, the result of our property system and our system of competition. One man owns a machine which does the work of five hundred men. Five hundred men are, in consequence, thrown out of employment, and having no work to do, become hungry and take to thieving. The one man secures the produce of the machine and keeps it, and has five hundred times as much as he should have, and probably, which is of much more importance, a great deal more than he really wants. Were that machine the property of all, every one would benefit by it. It would be an immense advantage to the community. All unintellectual labor, all monotonous, dull labor, all labor that deals with dreadful things, and involves unpleasant conditions, must be done by machinery. Machinery must work for us in coal mines, and do all sanitary services, and be the stoker of steamers, and clean the streets, and run messages on wet days, and do anything that is tedious or distressing. At present machinery competes against man. Under proper conditions machinery will serve man. There is no doubt at all that this is the future of machinery; and just as trees grow while the country gentleman is asleep, so while Humanity will be amusing itself, or enjoying cultivated leisure – which, and not labor, is the aim of man – or making beautiful things, or reading beautiful things, or simply contemplating the world with admiration and delight, machinery will be doing all the necessary and unpleasant work. The fact is, that civilization requires slaves. The Greeks were quite right there. Unless there are slaves to do the ugly, horrible, uninteresting work, culture and contemplation become almost impossible. Human slavery is wrong, insecure, and demoralizing. On mechanical slavery, on the slavery of the machine, the future of the world depends. And when scientific men are no longer called upon to go down to a depressing East End and distribute bad cocoa and worse blankets to starving people, they will have delightful leisure in which to devise wonderful and marvelous things for their own joy and the joy of every one else. There will be great storages of force for every city, and for every house if required, and this force man will convert into heat, light, or motion, according to his needs. Is this Utopian? A map of the world that does not include Utopia is not worth even glancing at, for it leaves out the one country at which Humanity is always landing. And when Humanity lands there, it looks out, and, seeing a better country, sets sail. Progress is the realization of Utopias.

Grand National Holiday

WILLIAM BENBOW, 1832

William Benbow was a rabble-rouser, pornographer and mysterious subversive, and his ideas have permeated into the history of resistance and revolt in Britain. When the Chartists tried to implement the National Holiday proposed by Benbow, he was jailed.

A holiday signifies a *holy* day, and ours is to be of holy days the most holy. It is to be most holy, most sacred, for it is to be consecrated to promote – to create rather – the happiness and liberty of mankind. Our holy day is established to establish plenty, to abolish want, to render all men equal! In our holy day we shall legislate for all mankind; the constitution drawn up during our holiday, shall place every human being on the same footing. Equal rights, equal liberties, equal enjoyments, equal toil, equal respect, equal share of production: this is the object of our holy day – of our sacred day – of our festival!

When a grand national holiday, festival, or feast is proposed, let none of our readers imagine that the proposal is new. It was an established custom among the Hebrews, the most ancient of people, to have holidays or festivals, not only religious feasts, but *political* ones. Their feasts were generally held to perpetuate the memory of God's mighty works; to allow the people frequent seasons for instruction in the laws, — to grant them time of rest, pleasure, and renovation of acquaintance with their brethren. The *Sabbath* was a weekly festival, not because they supposed that God reposed from his labor on that day, — but immemorial of their deliverance from Egypt, — out of the house of bondage, and of their feeding on manna in the wilderness. The true meaning of feeding on manna is, that the productions of the soil were equally divided among the people. They fed upon manna — that is they were fed in abundance. During the various festivals, no servile work was done, and servants and masters knew no distinction. Every seventh year, which was called the Year of Release, a continued festival was held among the Hebrews. Mark, a holiday for a whole year! How happy a people must be, how rich in provisions, to be able to cease from manual labor, and to cultivate their minds during the space of a whole year! We English must be in a pretty state, if in the midst of civilization and abundance, we cannot enjoy a month's holiday, and cease from labor during the short space of four weeks! But to return, — the Year of Release was a continued — unceasing festival; it was a season of instruction; it was a relief to poor debtors. The land lay untilled; the spontaneous produce was the property of the poor, the fatherless, and the widow; every debt was forgiven, and every bond-servant dismissed free, if he pleased, loaded with a variety of presents from his master. There was another holiday or feast deserving of mention; — it was called the *jubilee*. No servile work was done on it: the land lay untilled; what grew of itself belonged to the poor and needy; whatever debts the Hebrews owed to one another, were wholly remitted;

hired, as well as bond-servants, obtained their liberty; the holding of lands was changed, so that as the *jubilee* approached, the Hebrew lands bore the less price. By this means landed possession was not confined to particular families, and the sinful hastening to be rich was discouraged.

We have now shown that the holding of festivals is consecrated by divine authority; it only remains for us to show the necessity that there is for the people of this country holding one; and then to proceed to its details and object.

The grounds and necessity of our having a month's Holiday, arise from the circumstances in which we are placed. We are oppressed, in the fullest sense of the word; we have been deprived of every thing; we have no property, no wealth, and our labor is of no use to us, since what it produces goes into the hands of others. We have tried every thing but our own efforts; we have told our governors, over and over again, of our wants and misery; we thought them good and wise, and generous; we have for ages trusted to their promises, and we find ourselves, at this present day, after so many centuries of forbearance, instead of having our condition bettered, convinced that our total ruin is at hand. Our Lords and Masters have proposed no plan that we can adopt; they contradict themselves, even upon what they name the source of our misery. One says one thing, another says another thing. One scoundrel, one sacrilegious blasphemous scoundrel, says "that over-production is the cause of our wretchedness." Over-production, indeed! when we half-starving producers cannot, with all our toil, obtain any thing like a sufficiency of produce. It is the first time, that in any age or country, save our own, *abundance* was adduced as a cause of want. Good God!

where is this abundance? Abundance of food! ask the laborer and mechanic where they find it. Their emaciated frame is the best answer. Abundance of clothing! the nakedness, the shivering, the asthmas, the colds, and rheumatisms of the people, are proofs of the abundance of clothing! Our Lords and Masters tell us, we produce too much; very well then, we shall cease from producing for one month, and thus put into practice the theory of our Lords and Masters.

Over-population, our Lords and Masters say, is another cause of our misery. They mean by this, that the resources of the country are inadequate to its population. We must prove the contrary, and during a holiday take a census of the people, and a measurement of the land, and see upon calculation, whether it be not an unequal distribution, and a bad management of the land, that make our Lords and Masters say, that there are too many of us. Here are two strong grounds for our Holiday; for a CONGRESS of the working classes.

The greatest Captain of the age has acknowledged, that there was partial distress; Londonderry has said, that "ignorant impatience" was the cause of our misery; the sapient Robert Peel has asserted, that "our wants proceeded from our not knowing what we wanted." Very good; during our festival, we shall endeavor to put an end to partial distress; to get rid of our ignorant impatience, and to learn what it is we do want. And these are three other motives for holding a Congress of the working classes.

When Governments disagree; when they have a national right or interest to settle; a boundary to establish; to put an end to a war, or to prevent it; or when they combine to enslave, in order to be able to plunder the whole world, they hold a Congress. They send their wise men, their cunning men, to discuss, plan, and concoct what they call a treaty, and so, at least for a time, settle their differences. In this mode of proceeding there is something that we must imitate. In our National Holiday, which is to be held during one calendar month, throughout the United Kingdom of Great Britain and Ireland, we must all unite in discovering the source of our misery, and the best way of destroying it. Afterwards we must choose, appoint, and send to the place of Congress, a certain number of wise and cunning men, whom we shall have made fully acquainted with our circumstances; and they, before the Holiday be expired, shall discuss and concert a plan, whereby, if it is possible, the privation, wretchedness and slavery, of the great mass of us, may be diminished, if not completely annihilated.

We *affirm* that the state of society in this country is such, that as long as it continues, heart-rending inequality must continue, producing wretchedness, crime, and slavery; — plunging not a few, but the immense majority of the people into those abject circumstances. Our respect and love towards the human race in general, and more especially towards the working classes to whom we belong body and soul, has induced us to reflect and consider, and thus to discover what we think will bring about the object we aim at; namely, the happiness of the many. Our lords and masters, by their unity of thought and action, by their consultations, deliberations, discussions, holidays, and congresses, have up to this time succeeded in bringing about the happiness of the *few*. Can this be denied? We shall then by our consultations, deliberations, discussions, holidays, and congresses, endeavor to establish the happiness of the *immense majority* of the human race, of that far *largest portion*

called the *working classes*. What the few have done for themselves cannot the many do for themselves? Unquestion-
ably. Behold, O people and fellow laborers the way!

Before a month's holiday can take place, universal
preparations must be made for it. It should not take place
neither in seed-time nor in harvest-time. Every man must
prepare for it, and assist his neighbor in preparing for it.
The preparations must begin long before the time which
shall be hereafter appointed, in order that every one may
be ready, and that the festival be not partial but universal.

Committees of management of the working classes
must be forthwith formed in every city, town, village, and
parish throughout the United Kingdom. These committees must make themselves fully acquainted with the plan,
and be determined to use the extremest activity and perse-
verance to put into execution as speedily and effectually as
possible. They must call frequent meetings, and show the
necessity and object of the holiday. They must use every
effort to prevent intemperance of every sort, and recom-
mend the strictest sobriety and economy. The working
classes cannot lay in provisions for a month; this is not
wanted, but every man must do his best to be provided
with food for the first week of the holiday. Provisions for
the remaining three weeks can be easily procured. As for
wearing apparel, since the holiday will take place in the
summer, there can be no great difficulty in being provided
with sufficient covering for one month. If the committees
do their duty, and earnestly explain the nature and necessity of the holiday, they will induce all lovers of equal
rights, to make every sacrifice of momentary inconve-
nience in order to obtain permanent convenience and
comfort.

We suppose that the people are able to provide provisions and funds for one week; during this week they will be enabled to enquire into the funds of their respective cities, towns, villages and parishes, and to adopt means of having those funds, originally destined for their benefit, now applied to that purpose. The committee of management shall be required to direct the people in adopting the best measures that shall be deemed necessary. The people must be made aware of their own folly, in having allowed themselves to have been deceived by the Parish parsons, and Select Vestries, and they must cease permitting others to vote away their own money. The people, so soon as they shall see themselves in want of provisions or funds, must have immediate recourse to vestry meetings, which have power to grant, in despite of Overseers and Justices, such relief as may be wanted. There is nothing to prevent any six or ten persons from calling a vestry meeting as often as may be deemed requisite, and the registers, books, and other parish documents must be consulted, and will give sufficient evidence, that there is wherewithal to support the people during the holiday. Let it be constantly borne in mind, that the united voice of the people will be duly attended to, and that an equal division of funds and provisions will be allowed them by the parish authorities, when their object is known. The committee, which may also be looked upon as the commissary department, must likewise watch over the good order of its district, establish regularity, and punish all attempts at disorder. The people having a grand object in view, the slightest points in their character must be grand. About to renovate Europe, the people must appear renovated.

In the earlier periods of our history, monarchs, princes,

and rulers of minor titles, had recourse to voluntary loans. At first the people raised these loans voluntarily, for they thought by so doing, they would enable their chiefs to protect them. It was soon seen, however, that the voluntary loans were converted to the sole advantage of the chiefs, and their more immediate partisans, consequently the people began to grow slack in contributing them. By means of the voluntary loans, the chiefs or governors became powerful enough to exact involuntary loans, and the method of raising them was taxation, and other sorts of exaction. Hence, though sovereignty was at first supported by voluntary loans, as soon as it was discovered to be a self-interested institution, it was obliged to levy involuntary loans, that is, taxes. Now there is a species of sovereignty – we mean the sovereignty of the people – that has not as yet been supported, and it is for its support that we claim at this moment, during the festival that is to establish it, voluntary loans. When we talk of establishing the sovereignty of the people, we talk of establishing the grandeur, the happiness and liberty of the people. Nothing can be more deserving of praise and support. We have hitherto contributed to the sovereignty of particular families, that is to their grandeur, happiness and liberty; and their liberty must be called uncontrolled license – tyranny.

Now, since we have so long tried the sovereignty of particular families, let us try the sovereignty of the grand family – the human race. That species of sovereignty can never become tyranny. We call then upon every man to add his mite to this voluntary loan, and particularly the rich, who are always so generous in keeping up the splendor of ancient race. The antiquity of the human race they will not allow to be sullied by modern degradation. If they show pity and support towards the descendants of a Stuart, a Bourbon, or a Guelf, they will surely show more towards the descendants of Adam.

"The cattle upon a thousand hills are the Lord's." When the people's voice, which Lord Brougham proclaims to be the voice of God, and surely we need no higher legal authority, calls for its own, demands the cattle of the thousand hills, who dares withhold the cattle of the thousand hills? During our holiday the people may have need of this cattle: let them order it to the slaughterhouse, and their herdsmen and drovers will obey them. There may be some persons, who having been so long a time the keepers of the Lord's cattle, will be inclined to keep it still longer. However, we are of opinion, that when solicited they will render "unto the Lord that which is the Lord's." But there are other keepers of the people's cattle, whose unbounded liberality and strict probity are known to the whole world. These keepers may be classed under the denominations of Dukes, Marquesses, Earls, Lords, Barons, Baronets, Esquires, Justices, and Parsons, and they will all freely contribute to our glorious holiday. Some of them, according to the extent of the Lord's flocks, will send us a hundred sheep, others twenty oxen; loads of corn, vegetables, and fruit will be sent to each committee appointed by the Lord's voice, which, when distributed among the people, will enable them during the CONGRESS to legislate at their ease, without any fear of want tormenting any part of them.

Should there, however, be a few who may refuse to render up the Lord's cattle, the number of the greatly generous will infinitely counter-balance them. To the NEW-CASTLES, who think every thing their own, we will oppose the BURDETTS, who think all they possess, the Lord's or people's. What a faithful keeper of the Lord's cattle we shall find in Sir FRANCIS! The relief we shall obtain from him, when we wait upon him at Belper, Burton, and in Leicestershire, will be a proof of his generosity and probity. The following is the way Sir FRANCIS and all such honest keepers are to be waited on, and our wants and wishes made known to them. Although we name Sir FRANCIS, we do not give him any real preference over the Westminsters, the Russells, the Lansdownes, the Althorpes, &c. Let him, however, be supposed the keeper, that for form sake we are to wait upon. The Committee will depute 20 persons to wait upon Sir FRANCIS, and state to him respectfully, but energetically, their business. Suppose, but it is the most improbable of all suppositions, that Sir FRANCIS should not be inclined to pay full attention to the application. Then the Committee will send 100 persons, with the same request, urging it still more respectfully and energetically; and should there still be indifference on the part of Sir FRANCIS, the Committee shall send 1000 persons, and so on, increasing in proportion, until the Lord's cattle be forthcoming. The persons sent by the Committee, shall allow no one to disturb the peace of the people. Upon all visits from the Committee, the person visited must be seen in person by the Committee: not being at home is no excuse. Sir FRANCIS may be at Belper, Burton, or in Leicestershire; the Committee of those districts will find him at one or either of them, and solicit "England's glory" for support, which he will freely grant, as he is very rich, and very willing to establish the sovereignty, happiness, and liberty of the people.

Here be it observed, that the above mode of proceeding

is not limited to any part of the country, or to any one Sir FRANCIS. All the Sir FRANCISES, all the great reformers are to be applied to, and the people will have no longer any reason to suspect reformers' consistency. The reformers of the United Kingdom will hold out an open hand to support us during our festival. O'Connell will abandon the collection made for him; indeed that collection is virtually destined for our Irish brethren during the holiday. Until they are tried no one can imagine the number of great men ready to promote equal rights, equal justice, and equal laws all throughout the kingdom.

When all the details of the above plan are put into execution, the committee of each parish and district, shall select its wise men to be sent to the NATIONAL CONGRESS. A parish or district having a population of 15,000 four, a population of 25,000 eight, and London fifty wise and cunning men. The advice of the different committees is to be taken as to the most convenient place for conference. It should be a central position, and the mansion of some great liberal lord, with its out houses and appurtenances. The only difficulty of choice will be to fix upon a central one, for they are all sufficiently vast to afford lodging to the members of the Congress, their lands will afford nourishment, and their parks a beautiful place for meeting.

It may be relied upon, that the possessor of the mansion honored by the people's choice, will make those splendid preparations for the representatives of the sovereignty of the people, that are usually made for the reception of a common sovereign.

The object of the Congress; that is what it will have to do. To reform society, for "from the crown of our head to the sole of our foot there is no soundness in us." We must cut out the rottenness in order to become sound. Let us see what is rotten. Every man that does not work is rotten; he must be made work in order to cure his unsoundness. Not only is society rotten; but the land, property, and capital is rotting. There is not only something, but a great deal rotten in the state of England. Every thing, men, property, and money, must be put into a state of circulation. As the blood by stagnation putrefies, as it is impoverished by too much agitation, so society by too much idleness on the one hand, and too much toil on the other has become rotten. Every portion must be made work, and then the work will become so light, that it will not be considered work, but wholesome exercise. Can any thing be more humane than the main object of our glorious holiday, namely, to obtain for all at the least expense to all, the largest sum of happiness for all.

We think that the necessity of a GRAND NATIONAL HOLIDAY has been fully impressed upon the mind of every man who may have read us.

We have etched out the plan; not detailed and matured it, for it will take a longer time and deeper reflection before we can pronounce our plan complete. We expect the assistance of others, and we invite them, without putting us to unnecessary expense, to communicate to us their hints. We have explained in a few words our object: it will be seen that never was there an object, an aim so sublime, so full of humanity. We will not revert, now that we are forced to a conclusion, to the necessity of a holiday, but we must repeat ourselves respecting the plan.

We are sure that there is no one who will not be ready to join heart and hand in our festival, provided he can be persuaded of the possibility of holding it. If we had not been convinced of the possibility of holding it, we should never have mentioned it. All we require is that our holiday folk should be prepared for *one* week; we engage ourselves to provide for all their wants during the last three weeks of the festival. We have shown in what way the people should have recourse to vestry meetings, and what power they had over all parish authorities. We have shown that the parish authorities are entirely dependent on the people, and that without the consent of the people they can raise no rate, nor dispose of any fund already accumulated. We have shown that the people had a right to examine the parish accounts, and become cognizant of the funds held by the parish authorities, and that the people could dispose of those funds as they thought proper. If, then, there are funds in hand, the people will apply them to their own support during the holiday; if it should happen that there are not funds, the people must vote a supply, for the people must be convinced of one thing, namely that it is they alone who have a right of levying parish contributions. Some few persons may not like the idea of having recourse to parish allowance for their support even during the short period of three weeks, but these over-delicate individuals must reflect that they are becoming a *momentary* burden to their parish, in order to rid it of increasing, and *everlasting* burdens. We think we have said enough to prove, that by vestry meetings alone the people would be fully able to support themselves during the holiday. Let the people only reflect on the sums that the parish authorities have from time immemorial levied upon the people, without the concurrence of the people, and then they will have no longer any scruples, but will, if the occasion require it, have recourse to the same method for raising funds for the benefit of the many, that the few have always had for the benefit of the few. We are too honest, too conscientious, too delicate, consequently the few who are neither honest, conscientious nor delicate dupe us. We must avoid all squeamishness; we are not only working for ourselves but for the human race and its posterity. We beg of the people to throw off all false delicacy. They must boldly lay hands upon that which is their own.

We call our reader's attention to what we have said about "the cattle upon the thousand hills." They are the Lord's, that is the people's; and when the people want them, the guardians who have kept them so long, will deliver them unto the people. We repeat, and we do so expressly that the people may be the more convinced of what we assert, that Sir FRANCIS BURDETT, and all such liberal men, will come forward in shoals to support us. There is nothing enthusiastic or ideal in this assertion. Let us reflect upon it. Mr. COKE, of Norfolk, is a very rich man, and a very liberal man. Now we ask, what does a liberal man amass wealth for, if not in order to be able to support liberal principles. Mr. COKE's heart will beat with joy when he finds such an occasion for his liberality, as we are going to give him. We see him already ringing for his check-book, and ordering droves of his oxen, and waggon-loads of his wheat to be sent to us holiday folks. We hear him swearing at his servants, damning their laziness, when the demands of the people are to be satisfied. And in every county a COKE is to be found; in Middlesex you will find a BYNG, in Bedfordshire a WHITBREAD. It would be too long to mention names, but you have only to look over the list of the majority in the House of Commons on the Reform Bill, and the list of the minority in the House of Lords on the same Bill, and then you will see, at a glance, the number of liberal men who are keeping their riches for your advantage. Only think of the immense sums that these liberal men spend at elections, in order to legislate for you, and consequently do you good! Now can you be persuaded, that they will not liberally resist you when you are fighting your own battle. Be assured they will; not only will they send you funds and provisions, but you will find them simple volunteers in your ranks. HENRY BROUGHAM, Lord Chancellor, will, if you accept of him, volunteer his services as one of your Deputies to CONGRESS. These great men, O people, are waiting for you; as soon as they can rely upon you, you may rely upon them. All they want to declare themselves for you, is your support. Let them have it.

---

from *Future Work*
JAMES ROBERTSON, 1985

A vital voice on how we will work in the next millennium, the writing of James Robertson is aimed at putting the ethical back into the work ethic.

Leisure

As employment became the dominant form of work, the distinction between work and leisure became sharper. The word "leisure" means free time, and leisure activities came to mean what people did in the time they had to themselves, as contrasted with work which was what people did in the time claimed by their employer. This distinction between work and leisure has always been clearer for employees than for people who have organized their own work, like housewives or the self-employed.

This is linked with the fact that, in general, men in industrial societies have tended to enjoy more leisure than women.

Another distinction between work and leisure became sharper as employment became the dominant form of work. As work increasingly came to be activity which brought in money, so leisure increasingly came to be activity on which money had to be spent. A widening range of leisure industries and services grew up providing leisure goods and leisure facilities. Some of these were in the so-called private sector; people purchased leisure goods like hi-fis and services like package holidays from them directly. Others were in the so-called public sector; these were paid for out of public expenditure, financed by taxation, and the goods and services which they provided – like public swimming pools – were available to people free or at a reduced cost.

The shift from informal to formally organized work during the industrial age was thus paralleled by a comparable shift in the sphere of leisure. Whereas in pre-industrial societies most people organized leisure, like work, for themselves and one another, in late industrial societies they became dependent on the organizations of the formal economy to provide them with leisure activities as well as providing them with work.

One way of thinking about the future of leisure, as about the future of work, is to ask who controls people's time.

Employment has meant that employees lose control of their working time by selling it to their employers, and employers gain control of their employees' time by buying it from them. Something similar is true of leisure. As leisure industries and services have developed, people at leisure have increasingly spent their time on activities devised for them by others, including commercial organizations and public services. By contrast, in self-organized leisure – as in ownwork – people take control of the use of their own time. (There is, incidentally, a close connection between control over time and control over space. Employers normally control their employees' workspace, just as they control their worktime. Most employees have no workspace of their own. Similarly, leisure-providers normally control the space, as well as the time, used for leisure by their customers and clients.)

As people are required to spend less time in employment, they will have more time for leisure. The HE (Hyper-Expansionist) vision of post-industrial society foresees people spending most of this extra free time consuming leisure products and in leisure activities provided by leisure industries, leisure services and organized entertainment. People's leisure will be mainly outer-directed, just as their work has been outer-directed in employment. The SHE (Sane, Humane, Ecological) vision, on the other hand, foresees people using their increased free time in accordance with their own perceptions of value and need. The use they make of it will blur the distinction between leisure and ownwork.

Another way of thinking about the future of leisure is to distinguish between leisure activities that have to be paid for and leisure activities that do not – just as one way of thinking about the future of work is to distinguish between work that people get paid for and work that they do not. For example, there are leisure activities and facilities which cost a substantial amount of money. Foreign holidays are one example. Local authority sports centers are another. There are also leisure activities which cost comparatively little money, like walking or reading. Thirdly, there are leisure activities which save money. If you grow your own food and do your own repairs, you can eat better and live better for less money. Fourthly, there are leisure activities which can be turned into money-earning activities. Hobbies like photography and keeping chickens might be examples.

The Business-As-Usual view of the future of work assumes that leisure industries and services will continue to grow. The assumption is that people will still have jobs, and so will still have money to purchase leisure goods and services and to pay taxes and rates for public leisure facilities. The growth in this category of leisure is itself expected to be a source of new jobs.

The HE view assumes that many people will not have jobs, and will be dependent on being provided with leisure activities to fill their time. In this case, there would be a sharp distinction between the leisure-providers, who would be skilled and dedicated workers, and the consumers of leisure, who would play little part in providing or organizing leisure for themselves — just as, more generally, most people would play little part in meeting any of their own needs. The question of how these leisure activities would be financed, when many of the people enjoying them would not be earning incomes from employment, is one to which we shall return.

As already outlined, a change of direction towards ownwork and the SHE future will involve a shift of emphasis away from leisure industries and services to leisure organized by people for themselves. The dividing line between ownwork and this kind of leisure will often be difficult to draw. People will make use of their leisure – the increasing amount of time at their own disposal – to do useful work on their own account, on their own interests and on their own projects. Leisure activities will then shade into a much wider range of work and activity options than most people have today, when for most people leisure is what they have when not at work, and the two main options are either to work or to be unemployed.

---

from *The Gay Science*
FRIEDRICH NIETZSCHE, 1882

Whilst the more well-known aspects of Nietzschean thought, such as the Will to power and the übermensch, point to a philosophy of striving, this extract from one of his lesser-known works proves that he was not resistant to resting.

There is something in the American Indians, something of the ferocity peculiar to the Indian blood, in the American lust for gold; and the breathless haste with which they work – the distinctive vice of the new world – is already beginning to infect the old Europe with its ferocity and is spreading a lack of spirituality like a blanket. Even now one is ashamed of resting, and prolonged reflection almost gives people a bad conscience. One thinks with a watch in one's hand, even as one eats one's midday meal while reading the latest news of the stock market; one lives as if one "might miss out on something." "Rather do anything than nothing": this principle, too, is merely a string to throttle all culture and good taste. Just as all forms are visibly perishing by the haste of the workers, the feeling for form itself, the era and eye for the melody are also perishing. The proof of this may be found in the universal demand for gross obviousness in all those situations in which human beings wish to be honest with each other for once — in their associations with friends, women, relatives, children, teachers, pupils, leaders and princes: one no longer has the time and energy for ceremonies, for being obliging in a direct way, for *esprit* in conversation, and for any otium [leisure] at all. Living in a constant chase for gain compels people to expend their spirit to the point of exhaustion in continual pretense and overreaching and anticipating others. Virtue has come to consist of doing something in less time than someone else. Hours in which honesty is permitted have become rare, and when they arrive one is tired and does not only want to "let oneself go" but actually wishes to stretch out as long and wide and ungainly as one happens to be. This is how people now write letters, and the style of letters will always be the true "sign of the times."

If sociability and the arts still offer any delight, it is the kind of delight that slaves, weary of their work, devise for themselves. How frugal our educated — and uneducated — people have become regarding "joy"! How they are becoming increasingly suspicious of all joy! More and more, work enlists all good conscience on its side; the desire for joy already calls itself a "need to recuperate" and is beginning to be ashamed of itself. "One owes it to one's health" — that is what people say when they are caught on an excursion into the country. Soon we may well reach the point where people can no longer give in to the desire for a *vita contemplativa* (that is, taking a walk with ideas and friends) without self-contempt and a bad conscience.

Well, formerly it was the other way around: it was work

that was afflicted with the bad conscience. A person of good family used to conceal the fact that he was working if need compelled him to work. Slaves used to work, oppressed by the feeling that they were doing something contemptible. "Nobility and honor are attached solely to otium and bellum [war]," that was the ancient prejudice.

from *The Right to be Lazy*
PAUL LAFARGUE, 1883

This second excerpt from The Right to be Lazy *exposes the ancient philosopher's abhorrence of work. Published in the heyday of Socialist uprising, this tract advocating less work was a bestseller.*

Appendix

Our moralists are very modest people. If they invented the dogma of work, they still have doubts of its efficacy in tranquilizing the soul, rejoicing the spirit, and maintaining the proper functioning of the entrails and other organs. They wish to try its workings on the populace, *in anima vili*, before turning it against the capitalists, to excuse and authorize whose vices is their peculiar mission.

But, you, three-for-a-cent philosophers, why thus cudgel your brains to work out an ethics the practice of which you dare not counsel to your masters? Your dogma of work, of which you are so proud, do you wish to see it scoffed at, dishonored? Let us open the history of ancient peoples and the writings of their philosophers and law givers. "I could not affirm," says the father of history, Herodotus, "whether the Greeks derived from the Egyptians the contempt which they have for work, because I find the same contempt established among the Thracians, the Cythians, the Persians, the Lydians; in a word, because among most barbarians, those who learn mechanical arts and even their children are regarded as the meanest of their citizens. All the Greeks have been nurtured in this principle, particularly the Lacedaemonians."[1]

"At Athens the citizens were veritable nobles who had to concern themselves but with the defense and the administration of the community, like the savage warriors from whom they descended. Since they must thus have all their time free to watch over the interests of the republic, with their mental and bodily strength, they laid all labor upon the slaves. Likewise at Lacedaemon, even the women were not allowed to spin or weave that they might not detract from their nobility."[2]

The Romans recognized but two noble and free professions, agriculture and arms. All the citizens by right lived at the expense of the treasury without being constrained to provide for their living by any of the sordid arts (thus, they designated the trades), which rightfully belonged to slaves. The elder Brutus to arouse the people, accused Tarquin, the tyrant, of the special outrage of having converted free citizens into artisans and masons.[3]

The ancient philosophers had their disputes upon the origin of ideas but they agreed when it came to the abhorrence of work. "Nature," said Plato in his social utopia, his model republic, "Nature has made no shoemaker nor smith. Such occupations degrade the people who exercise them. Vile mercenaries, nameless wretches, who are by

[1] Herodotus, Book II
[2] Biot, *De L'abolition de L'esclavage ancien en Occident*, 1840
[3] Livy, Book I

their very condition excluded from political rights. As for the merchants accustomed to lying and deceiving, they will be allowed in the city only as a necessary evil. The citizen who shall have degraded himself by the commerce of the shop shall be prosecuted for this offense. If he is convicted, he shall be condemned to a year in prison; the punishment shall be doubled for each repeated offense."[4]

In his "Economics," Xenophon writes, "The people who give themselves up to manual labor are never promoted to public offices, and with good reason. The greater part of them, condemned to be seated the whole day long, some even to endure the heat of the fire continually, cannot fail to be changed in body, and it is almost inevitable that the mind be affected." "What honorable thing can come out of a shop?" asks Cicero. "What can commerce produce in the way of honor? Everything called shop is unworthy of an honorable man. Merchants can gain no profit without lying, and what is more shameful than falsehood? Again, we must regard as something base and vile the trade of those who sell their toil and industry, for whoever gives his labor for money sells himself and puts himself in the rank of slaves."[5]

Proletarians, brutalized by the dogma of work, listen to the voice of these philosophers, which has been concealed from you with jealous care: A citizen who gives his labor for money degrades himself to the rank of slaves, he commits a crime which deserves years of imprisonment.

Christian hypocrisy and capitalist utilitarianism had not perverted these philosophers of the ancient republics.

---

[4] Plato, *Republic*, Book V
[5] Cicero, *De officiis*, I, 42

Speaking for free men, they expressed their thought naively. Plato, Aristotle, those intellectual giants, beside whom our latter day philosophers are but pygmies, wish the citizens of their ideal republics to live in the most complete leisure, for as Xenophon observed, "Work takes all the time and with it one has no leisure for the republic and his friends." According to Plutarch, the great claim of Lycurgus, wisest of men, to the admiration of posterity, was that he had granted leisure to the citizens of Sparta by forbidding to them any trade whatever. But our moralists of Christianity and capitalism will answer, "These thinkers and philosophers praised the institution of slavery." Perfectly true, but could it have been otherwise, granted the economic and political conditions of their epoch? War was the normal state of ancient societies. The free man was obliged to devote his time to discussing the affairs of state and watching over its defense. The trades were then too primitive and clumsy for those practicing them to exercise their birth-right of soldier and citizen; thus the philosophers and lawgivers, if they wished to have warriors and citizens in their heroic republics, were obliged to tolerate slaves. But do not the moralists and economists of capitalism praise wage labor, the modern slavery; and to what men does the capitalist slavery give leisure? To people like Rothschild, Schneider, and Madame Boucicaut, useless and harmful slaves of their vices and of their domestic servants. "The prejudice of slavery dominated the minds of Pythagoras and Aristotle," — this has been written disdainfully; and yet Aristotle foresaw: that if every tool could by itself execute its proper function, as the masterpieces of Daedalus moved themselves or as the tripods of Vulcan set themselves spontaneously at their sacred work; if for example the shuttles of the weavers did their own weaving, the foreman of the workshop would have no more need of helpers, nor the master of slaves.

Aristotle's dream is our reality. Our machines, with breath of fire, with limbs of unwearying steel, with fruitfulness, wonderfully inexhaustible, accomplish by themselves with docility their sacred labor. And nevertheless the genius of the great philosophers of capitalism remains dominated by the prejudice of the wage system, worst of slaveries. They do not yet understand that the machine is the savior of humanity, the god who shall redeem man from the *sordidae artes* and from working for hire, the god who shall give him leisure and liberty.

---

from *Capitalism, Socialism, Ecology*
ANDRÉ GORZ, 1991

Work has changed, and the workers have changed too.
    We may ask what proportion of the workforce
    would still define their identity in terms of their
    work and their working lives.
Or what proportion still regard their work as the focus
of their lives.

A Sane Revolution
from *Pansies*

D.H. LAWRENCE, 1928–29

If you make a revolution, make it for fun.
don't make it in ghastly seriousness,

don't do it in deadly earnest,
do it for fun.

Don't do it because you hate people,
do it just to spit in their eye.

Don't do it for the money,
do it and be damned to the money.

Don't do it for equality,
do it because we've got too much equality
and it would be fun to upset the apple-cart
and see which way the apples would go a-rolling.

Don't do it for the working classes.
Do it so that we can all of us be little aristocracies on
    our own
and kick our heels like jolly escaped asses.

Don't do it, anyhow, for international Labor.
Labor is the one thing a man has had too much of.
Let's abolish labor, let's have done with laboring!
Work can be fun, and men can enjoy it; then it's not
    labor.
Let's have it so! Let's make a revolution for fun!

ABOUT THE EDITORS

TOM HODGKINSON was born in 1968. After graduating from university he worked for a year in a skateboard shop. Later, he worked lazily and unhappily on a tabloid magazine for two years, and was fortunately fired. While on the dole, he confronted his guilt about not working by setting up a magazine called *The Idler* with his friend Gavin Pretor-Pinney. He is still unsuccessfully trying to avoid work.

MATTHEW DE ABAITUA was born in 1971, raised in Liverpool and lowered in London. He is Deputy Editor of *The Idler* magazine and has written for *Esquire*, the *Guardian*, and the *Observer*. He came to idleness through a series of menial jobs including security guard, barman, income support claimant, and stand-up comedian.